Lamingtons
& Lemon Tart

For Cath

Lamingtons & Lemon Tart

BEST-EVER CAKES, DESSERTS & TREATS
FROM A MODERN SWEETS MAESTRO

DARREN PURCHESE

hardie grant books

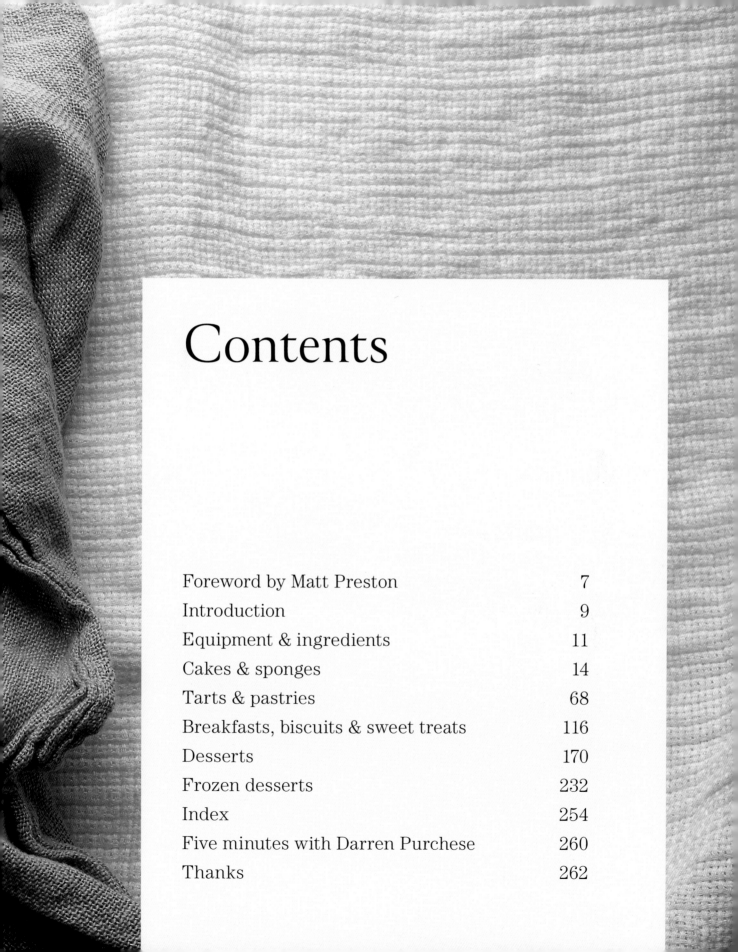

Contents

Foreword

'This is a book all about technical exactitude and the search for amazing flavour. It will challenge you; it will at times confound you; but it will also reward you with desserts that are as much a work of art as they are a riot of texture and flavour.'

Well, actually it is not; that was Darren's last book.

This one, the evocatively titled *Lamingtons & Lemon Tart*, is different. It's about recipes you'll want to cook immediately – well, perhaps after you've lasciviously devoured Patricia Niven's moody pictures of Darren's sweets in various states of dress and undress.

Sure, all the cakes, desserts, tarts and pastries here bang with flavour, but the recipes in *this* book won't take 2 days to make, and the taste combinations are as warm and familiar as a hug from your favourite aunt – pear, hazelnut and chocolate; raspberry, lychee and rose; almond, nectarine and fig; bitter chocolate and orange. Although, I should note that as this is Darren, you must expect the occasional pumpkin ice cream or avocado cream to sneak its way into recipes. He just can't help himself.

You also won't need ninja-like skills to pull them off this time because Darren has come down from the lofty pastry peak where he normally resides at Melbourne's divine Burch & Purchese to share his not inconsiderable wisdom about how to make everything from the best sponge, tart or éclair to his salted caramel and milk chocolate cake or decadent cherry almond cheesecake. Damn, just writing that I swear I put on 5 kilograms.

Think of Darren as a cross between Yoda, a Michelin-starred pastry chef and a sharp-eyed grandmother who has a sofa upholstered in country-show baking ribbons – but with better hair. Oh, and he's not green.

To further help you achieve baking brilliance, Darren has included step-by-step photo instructions for making everything from jellies and Swiss rolls to tempering chocolate.

You will find desserts of all forms here, although, in Darren's world, everything can be turned into a dessert. In the very first recipe, Jamaican ginger cake, he suggests serving it with caramelised white chocolate ice cream, providing the perfect recipe. This sets the tone for the whole tome; if there is some way to make something more delicious, more decadent, more 'OMG, how did you do that Mum/Dad/Son/Uncle Pete!!!', Darren will show you a sure-fire and eminently achievable way to do it. Even if this revolves around hiding a sponge cake inside a glazed cushion of white chocolate mousse – which is about the best idea I've heard since Charles Manly told me how he'd constructed a 5-cylinder water-cooled radial engine based on Stephen Balzer's rotary engines.

So dive in and prepare to be entertained, amazed and driven into the kitchen with uncontrollable desire to bake, roll, set and glaze. I suspect your personal satisfaction will be immense, but more importantly your friends and family will thank you for it!

Mwah!

Matt Preston

Introduction

I want to let you into a secret. I am making myself more accessible. Yes, I'm known as the chef with the tricks, with a scientific approach to food and ingredients. That's right, the chef armed with the latest kitchen gadgetry and a modern kitchen in which I execute my elaborate designs. I'm not like this *all* the time though. When I'm at home or entertaining close friends or family, it's the simpler, comforting style of food that I return to again and again.

I have been extremely lucky to have enjoyed an amazing career as a pastry chef and I've cooked in some pretty special places and prestigious kitchens around the world. From a restaurant set in the picturesque French Alps, to the iconic Savoy Hotel on London's Strand, from a kitchen at the Sydney Opera House with a window overlooking the Sydney Harbour Bridge, to the finest restaurants in Melbourne, I have worked at the high end of things.

It was at these places that I built my reputation for amazing, technically difficult cakes and desserts that deliver on taste as well as presentation. I am often the guy asked to produce the incredible dessert or the ridiculously tricky 'pressure test' for television cooking shows. So you may have an opinion that the food I love to eat is hard to replicate or will have too many steps to be practical to make. You may also wonder what I eat and enjoy in my spare time and what my idea of dessert heaven would be. This book has the answers to those questions and more.

My preferred desserts are the achievable, classic crowd-pleasers. What could be better than an ice cream sandwich on a hot day, or salted caramel dripping over a sponge? Do you love the oozing centre of a perfectly cooked chocolate fondant, and do you lick the spoon when making your favourite cake? I do. In fact, I probably love exactly the same things as you.

I have now written a cookbook that everyone can use. Whether it is the classic Australian chocolate and coconut lamington, a perfectly tangy lemon tart, the definitive nutty chocolate brownie, a 'go-to' chocolate birthday cake or my addictive salted caramel, this book has something for all levels of home cooks – plus plenty to keep more advanced chefs happy. And guess what? You don't need fancy equipment and very little in the way of out-of-the-ordinary ingredients.

If your mind is not blown by the ease of some of these dishes, then the flavour will surely knock you out. The recipes in this book are truly my favourites. Some are classics and some are my own inventions, and hopefully you will love them as much as I do. I guess people come to my shop to buy the things they can't make themselves but, with this book, that is exactly what you can do. Enjoy.

Darren Purchese

Equipment & ingredients

I have tried to make the recipes in this book as achievable as possible. Hopefully you will have most of the equipment needed or at least suitable alternatives. Following are a few useful notes about the most important tools you'll need, plus suggestions for substitutions. As with the equipment side of things, as much as possible, I have used ingredients that are easily found. There will be a few exceptions, but I will steer you in the direction of a source or substitute.

OVEN

All oven cooking temperatures are for fan-forced ovens. For conventional ovens, increase the temperature by 20°C (35°F).

TRAYS, TINS AND RINGS

Most of the cake tins, loaf (bar) tins, baking trays and similar, which are called for in the recipes are pretty straightforward. I obtained standard sizes of these from my local supermarket to ensure you have the best chance of recreating my work. All of the tins and trays were non-stick – this is not essential, though, and you may already own a suitable-sized tray or tin that isn't non-stick. If so, just make sure you line it with baking paper and grease it with canola spray. I have given dimensions for all the equipment. Try to stick as closely as possible to these when making the recipes, but you can, of course, bake your brownie in a square tin rather than a loaf tin and cook your ginger cake in something other than the suggested cake tin.

For the cannelé I used individual copper cannelé moulds, which can be extremely expensive. However, there is an alternative. I found a non-stick cannelé tray in a cookware store, which worked just as well as my copper ones, so I would recommend seeking out one of these if you plan on making this recipe. A quick search online would be recommended if you can't find one.

For the madeleines I used a silicone mat with 16 indents. There are plenty of these available in varying sizes and number of indents. I find the silicone ones easier to use than traditional metal madeleine trays, which can sometimes stick. The beautiful madeleines in the photo were cooked in a domestic oven in an inexpensive silicone mat.

Some recipes in the book call for metal pastry or cake rings, such as the Roasted pineapple pancakes, the Cherry and almond cheesecake and the Coconut raspberry sponge with white chocolate and vanilla mousse. These are rings with no base and are great for setting mousses in, cooking in or just to keep things a uniform shape. They need greasing or lining with baking paper or plastic wrap and can be found in specialist cookware stores. I actually get mine online and find them a handy addition to my kitchen, as they are useful for many different things.

POTS AND PANS

All of the pots and pans used in this book are from my domestic collection. I tested all the recipes at home, so really only used what I would normally have on hand. I have a large, medium and small-stainless steel pan collection and sometimes use a large cast-iron pan.

THERMOMETER

You really need one of these to ensure accurate temperatures for the recipes in this book and for the best results. They are fairly inexpensive but they can really help you out. Chocolate work, caramel, confectionery and syrups, as well as other bits and pieces, will all have a great chance of turning out as intended if you can check temperatures precisely. There are two types of thermometer available. One is a glass sugar thermometer and the other is a digital thermometer with a metal probe end. Both have multiple uses but only the digital one will cover all bases for this book. The digital thermometer is ideal for chocolate and easy to clean as well as read. It is inexpensive and an essential tool for your kitchen. Thermometers can be found in cookware shops, ingredient shops, some supermarkets and also online.

ICE CREAM MACHINE

There are recipes in this book for frozen desserts. Some of these only need a freezer but some do require an ice cream churner. Please read the manufacturer's instructions for your particular machine to ensure you get the best results. If you require ice cream for a recipe and you don't have an ice cream churning machine, or don't want to go to the trouble of making your own, it is entirely acceptable for you to buy one of the excellent ice cream brands on the market these days.

MICROWAVE

I don't have a fancy microwave. It was a cheap one from a department store and it lives in my house and is used every day. I would recommend investing in glass Pyrex-style microwave dishes with adjustable steam-release lids, as these are great for cooking apples. My wife, Cath, also makes a mean tomato sauce in them. I use glass bowls for melting chocolate at home but plastic are probably better if you can find them, as glass retains heat for longer.

SMALL EQUIPMENT

Some inexpensive smaller items that you might want to consider adding to your collection of kitchen tools are:

MICROPLANE Great for final touches of zesting citrus into mixes. It's finer than using the small side of a cheese grater and far more satisfying to use.

PASTRY BRUSH This is good for brushing syrups onto sponges and for brushing egg washes onto pastry.

SILICONE SPATULA Great for mixing, scraping and scooping creams into piping (icing) bags. These are heat resistant, which allows you to cook with them directly on the stove top when stirring hot mixtures.

SMALL STEP PALETTE KNIFE Called 'step' or 'crank' handled because of the step shape of the design, this palette knife helps you to pick up pastry items easily.

SMALL STRAINERS AND A LARGER SIEVE The smaller strainers are for passing small quantities of liquids, such as jelly mixes, into jugs and for dusting icing (confectioners') sugar or cocoa powder onto cakes for finishing. The larger sieve is for straining larger quantities of liquids and for sifting larger quantities of flours into bowls for baking.

EGGS

I use medium-sized eggs around 55–60 g (about 2 oz) per egg with the yolk being around 20 g (¾ oz) and the white being around 35 g (1¼ oz). For the recipes in this book, eggs should be at room temperature when you use them, as they will produce better results. When making meringue, egg whites that are old will work better than fresh – I like my whites to be around a week old for meringue.

CREAM

I use the same cream for all cooking applications throughout this book. It is a thickened (whipping) cream, found everywhere, containing 35 per cent butterfat. It is great for whipping and cooking. In some recipes I call for cream to be served with dishes such as crumble or brownie. For this you can use thicker or a thinner style cream as you wish.

CHOCOLATE

Chocolate is an extremely important ingredient to me. I use it every day in everything from sponges and mousses to garnishes and sauces. Basically, the higher-quality chocolate that you can afford will result in a higher-quality finished product, so try to choose wisely. Some are better than others so please check the packaging to ensure there is no vegetable oil present, as that is a sure sign of an inferior-quality product. I use Callebaut Belgian chocolate for recipes that require dark chocolate, which contains around 60 per cent cocoa solids.

SUGAR SYRUP

Sugar syrup is called for throughout this book and it is super-easy to make. Simply place equal quantities of caster (superfine) sugar and water in a saucepan and mix well with a spoon. Place the saucepan over medium heat and slowly bring the syrup to the boil. Cook the syrup for a minute or so, until the sugar has dissolved, then remove the pan from the heat. Leave the pan to cool at room temperature before straining the syrup into a plastic container and storing in the refrigerator until needed. The syrup will last for up to 2 weeks in the refrigerator.

FREEZE-DRIED FRUIT

This is a relatively new ingredient used in cooking, but I love to use it as a garnish on many of my cakes, desserts and sweet creations. You can find this product in specialist ingredient shops and I have seen them in some supermarkets. Burch & Purchese sells the Fresh-As brand of freeze-dried fruit, and you can order them direct online.

CHAPTER ONE

Cakes
& Sponges

Cake anybody? This chapter includes some of the simplest yet most delicious recipes in the book – from a moist, fudgy brownie to a ginger cake that's perfect with a cuppa. The salted caramel and milk chocolate cake and the twist on a classic Victoria sponge are sure to become favourites. There's also a coconut raspberry sponge with an ace white chocolate mousse and a new-school raspberry jelly. Hopefully you'll enjoy them as much as I do and they will become almost like members of your family, coming together for all the important occasions. Remember, bakers gonna bake.

JAMAICAN GINGER CAKE WITH CARAMELISED WHITE CHOCOLATE ICE CREAM

Serves 8–10

COMPONENTS
> Jamaican ginger cake
> Caramelised white chocolate
  ice cream

Just simply a great ginger cake that's a cinch to make. You can have it with or without the ice cream – it's up to you. This spicy sponge also goes well with my tangy lemon curd (see page 78) as well as a host of other things.

JAMAICAN GINGER CAKE

140 g (5 oz) unsalted butter
140 g (5 oz) soft light brown sugar
140 g (5 oz) black treacle (molasses)
finely grated zest of 1 orange
finely grated zest of 1 lemon
210 g (7½ oz) plain (all-purpose)
  flour (cake or soft flour if you can
  find it)
20 g (¾ oz) ground ginger
5 g (¼ oz) ground cinnamon
pinch of freshly ground black pepper
pinch of salt
5 g (¼ oz) bicarbonate of soda
  (baking soda)
2 eggs
170 ml (5½ fl oz/⅔ cup) full-cream
  (whole) milk

Preheat the oven to 165°C (330°F). Grease an 18 cm (7 in) non-stick cake tin with a removable base.

Place the butter, sugar and treacle in a large heavy-based saucepan over medium heat. Stir the mixture constantly until the butter has melted and the sugar has dissolved.

Remove the pan from the heat and add in the citrus zests. Allow the mixture to cool for 10 minutes.

Sift the flour with the spices, salt and bicarbonate of soda into a bowl and stir in the cooled butter and sugar mixture. Mix well to remove any lumps. Add the eggs to the bowl, one by one, stirring well after each addition. Mix well for a minute then add the milk and mix again thoroughly to incorporate.

Pour the batter into the greased tin and bake for 40 minutes or until the sponge is cooked. To test to see if the sponge is cooked, insert a skewer into the centre and pull it out. If it comes out clean the sponge is cooked through.

Allow the cake to cool then remove it from the tin.

> TIP: This cake freezes well. Wrap it in plastic wrap and place it in the freezer for up to 2 months. >

CARAMELISED WHITE CHOCOLATE ICE CREAM

100 g (3½ oz) Caramelised white chocolate (see page 177), cooled and roughly chopped
250 ml (8½ fl oz/1 cup) full-cream (whole) milk
150 ml (5 fl oz) thickened (whipping) cream
2 vanilla beans, seeds scraped
80 g (2¾ oz/⅓ cup) caster (superfine) sugar
5 egg yolks

Place the chocolate in a bowl.

Place the milk, cream, vanilla seeds and pods in a saucepan. Bring the mixture to a simmer over medium heat then remove the pan from the heat. Set the mixture aside and discard the vanilla pods.

In a mixing bowl, whisk the sugar and egg yolks together until they start to thicken and pale.

Pour one-third of the hot milk mixture into the sugar and egg mixture and mix well with a whisk. Pour this mixture back into the saucepan with the remaining hot milk mixture and mix well with a spatula or wooden spoon.

Place the pan back over medium–low heat and stir constantly until the mixture reaches a temperature of 82°C (180°F). Use a sugar or digital thermometer to check the temperature accurately.

Remove the custard from the heat and pour it over the chocolate in the bowl. Stir to emulsify and melt the chocolate. Place the bowl in a larger bowl of iced water to cool the custard down quickly, stirring regularly.

Once cool, churn in an ice cream machine according to the manufacturer's instructions. Store in the freezer until needed.

> TIP: You can make the ice cream base up to 4 days in advance, but try to churn it on the day of serving to achieve the best possible result.

TO SERVE

icing (confectioners') sugar for dusting
finely grated orange zest

While still warm, dust the cake with icing sugar mixed with finely grated orange zest. Serve warm with the ice cream.

LIGHT CARROT CAKE

Serves 10–12

3 eggs
250 g (9 oz) brown sugar
200 g (7 oz/1⅓ cups) plain (all-
  purpose) flour
2 teaspoons baking powder
1 teaspoon bicarbonate of soda
  (baking soda)
1 teaspoon ground nutmeg
1 teaspoon ground cinnamon
1 teaspoon ground ginger
350 g (12½ oz) carrots, roughly
  grated
140 g (5 oz) sultanas (golden raisins)
100 g (3½ oz) walnuts, chopped
100 ml (3½ fl oz) olive oil
finely grated zest of 1 orange

Sometimes it is the simplest things in life that give us the most pleasure. Delicious with a cup of tea, this cake is a little lighter in texture than a traditional carrot cake and is an absolute breeze to make. The spices and zest are the perfect match for sweet carrots and bitter walnuts.

Preheat the oven to 165°C (330°F). Spray a 28 x 13 x 6.5 cm (11 x 5 x 2½ in) loaf (bar) tin with canola oil and line with a strip of baking paper to cover the length of the tin, plus overlap of a couple of centimetres (about an inch) either side. Spray the paper with canola oil.

Place the eggs and sugar in a mixing bowl and whisk with an electric mixer on medium speed for 10 minutes or until thick and pale.

Sift the flour, baking powder, bicarbonate of soda and spices into a bowl.

Fold the egg mixture into the flour mixture by hand, using a spatula. Mix in the carrots, sultanas and walnuts, and finally the oil and orange zest.

Transfer the batter to the prepared tin and smooth it into the corners using a spatula. Bake in the oven for 40 minutes or until cooked through. To test to see if the cake is cooked, insert a skewer into the centre and pull it out. If it comes out clean the cake is cooked through.

Serve the cake warm. I find a cup of Earl Grey works very well served with a slice of this cake, as the bergamot flavour complements the orange in the cake.

BANANA, CHOCOLATE AND MANGO BREAD WITH CHOCOLATE ICE CREAM

Serves 10–12

COMPONENTS
> Banana, chocolate and
  mango bread
> Chocolate ice cream

Everyone has a banana bread recipe but I want you to give this one a go. The addition of mango works so well for flavour and colour, but you could make this with banana only if you want. Just use a total of 520 g (1 lb 2 oz) banana flesh and omit the mango. Oh – and it has chocolate in it and it's delicious. You need this in your life!

BANANA, CHOCOLATE AND MANGO BREAD

380 g (13½ oz) plain (all-purpose)
  flour
1 teaspoon salt
1 teaspoon bicarbonate of soda
  (baking soda)
1 teaspoon ground nutmeg
220 g (8 oz) unsalted butter,
  melted
385 g (13½ oz) caster (superfine)
  sugar
2 vanilla beans, seeds scraped
3 eggs
320 g (11½ oz) overripe banana
  flesh, mashed with a fork
200 g (7 oz) mango flesh, blitzed
  to a purée in a blender
200 g (7 oz) dark chocolate,
  roughly chopped

Preheat the oven to 160°C (320°F). Line a 28 x 13 x 6.5 cm (11 x 5 x 2½ in) loaf (bar) tin with baking paper and spray it with canola oil.

Sift the flour, salt, bicarbonate of soda and nutmeg into a bowl.

Beat the melted butter, sugar and vanilla seeds with an electric mixer for 10 minutes on high speed. Reduce the speed to medium and add the eggs one at a time, beating well after each addition. Mix for 5 minutes before adding the banana and mango. Mix for a further minute.

Mix in the dry ingredients using a spatula and add the chocolate. Mix again to combine before turning the mixture into the prepared tin. Smooth and flatten with a small spatula or spoon.

Bake in the oven for 1 hour or until the top of the loaf is golden brown and it is cooked through. To test to see if the banana bread is cooked, insert a skewer into the centre and pull it out. If it comes out clean the banana bread is cooked through.

Remove from the oven and allow the bread to cool for 30 minutes in the tin before turning it out onto a wire rack to cool completely. Serve immediately or wrap up for later. >

CHOCOLATE ICE CREAM

400 ml (13½ fl oz) full-cream
(whole) milk
70 ml (2¼ fl oz) thickened
(whipping) cream
85 g (3 oz) caster (superfine) sugar
3 egg yolks
70 g (2½ oz) dark chocolate, melted

Place the milk and cream in a saucepan over medium–low heat and bring to a simmer. Remove the pan from the heat and set aside.

In a mixing bowl, whisk the sugar and egg yolks together until they start to thicken and pale.

Pour one-third of the hot milk mixture into the yolk and sugar mixture and whisk well to combine.

Pour this mixture back into the saucepan with the remaining milk and stir well with a spatula or wooden spoon to combine.

Place the pan back over medium heat and stir constantly while cooking the ice cream base to 82°C (180°F). Use a digital or sugar thermometer for accuracy.

Remove the custard from the heat and mix in the melted chocolate. Strain the mixture into a bowl. Set this bowl into a larger bowl of iced water to cool the custard down quickly, stirring regularly.

Once cool, churn in an ice cream machine according to the manufacturer's instructions. Store the ice cream in the freezer until needed.

> TIP: You can make the ice cream base up to 4 days in advance but try to churn the ice cream on the day of serving for the best result.

TO SERVE

Slice the banana, chocolate and mango bread and serve with a dollop of the chocolate ice cream.

> TIP: You might like to check out the recipe on page 203, which gives you some ideas on how to 'pimp up' this banana bread and transform it into a spectacular dessert.

SALTED CARAMEL AND
MILK CHOCOLATE CAKE
WITH SALTED CARAMEL CREAM

Serves 8–10

COMPONENTS
> Salted caramel cream
> Salted caramel and milk
  chocolate cake

I wanted to include a few of my go-to, tried-and-tested recipes in this book. As much as I am known for cakes and desserts with multiple components and layers, when I cook at home I often return to simpler recipes that I know will be crowd-pleasers – and this is one of them. It's an easy method and a cake that really showcases one of my favourite ingredients. Yep, you guessed it … salted caramel.

The salted caramel cream is a great recipe, useful for spreading or piping and much better than just using regular salted caramel, which can leak and tear the cake when spreading it too cold.

SALTED CARAMEL CREAM

185 ml (6 fl oz) thickened
  (whipping) cream
225 g (8 oz) caster (superfine) sugar
4 eggs
2 gold-strength gelatine leaves
  (4 g/¼ oz) , soaked and drained
  (see page 33)
1 teaspoon salt
165 g (6 oz) unsalted butter

Place the cream in a saucepan and bring to the boil over medium heat, then remove the pan from the heat and set aside.

Place a larger saucepan over medium heat for 1 minute until hot. Gradually add the sugar to the pan in three stages. Stir with a wooden spoon or heat-resistant spatula to dissolve the sugar, and cook each addition until it is a deep amber colour before you add the next batch.

Once all the sugar is in and you have a golden caramel, add half the hot cream. BE CAREFUL! This mixture will expand furiously and the steam is extremely hot. Whisk the mixture and gradually add the remaining cream until everything is combined.

Once the mixture has settled, whisk the eggs in a bowl by hand. Pour over one-third of the cream mixture and continue to mix well.

Pour this mixture back into the saucepan and again stir to combine. Reduce the heat to low and cook the mixture until it reaches a temperature of 82°C (180°F). Use a sugar or digital thermometer for accuracy. Remove the pan from the heat.

Whisk the gelatine into the pan, along with the salt and butter, until you have a smooth cream. Pour the cream into a container and cool for a minimum of 4 hours before using. >

SALTED CARAMEL AND MILK CHOCOLATE CAKE

160 g (5½ oz) caster (superfine) sugar

120 ml (4 fl oz) thickened (whipping) cream

120 g (4½ oz) cold unsalted butter, diced

1 tablespoon liquid glucose

1 vanilla bean, seeds scraped

1 teaspoon salt

210 g (7½ oz) plain (all-purpose) flour (cake or soft flour if you can find it)

1 teaspoon bicarbonate of soda (baking soda)

2 eggs

120 ml (4 fl oz) full-cream (whole) milk

120 g (4½ oz) milk chocolate, roughly chopped

Preheat the oven to 160°C (320°F). Grease an 18 cm (7 in) non-stick cake tin with a removable base.

Place a large saucepan over medium heat for 1 minute until hot. Gradually add the sugar to the pan in three stages. Stir with a wooden spoon or heat-resistant spatula to dissolve the sugar and cook each addition until it is a deep amber colour before you add the next batch.

Once all the sugar is in and you have a golden caramel, add the cream, butter, glucose, vanilla seeds and salt. Stir well until you have a thick, golden, even-coloured caramel. Turn off the heat and leave to cool in the pan for 20 minutes.

Sift the flour and bicarbonate of soda into the bowl of a freestanding electric mixer then mix in the cooled caramel. Attach the paddle and mix on medium speed to remove any lumps and gradually add the eggs, one at a time, until both are incorporated. Mix well for 1 minute. Add the milk and chocolate and mix well to incorporate.

Pour the batter into the prepared tin and bake for 30–40 minutes, or until the cake is cooked. To test to see if the cake is cooked, insert a skewer into the centre and pull it out. If it comes out clean the cake is cooked through.

Allow the cake to cool in the tin then turn it out.

> TIP: This cake freezes well. Wrap it in plastic wrap and place it in the freezer for up to 2 months.

ASSEMBLY

Dutch (unsweetened) cocoa powder for dusting

Transfer the cooled caramel cream to a mixing bowl and smooth out using a spatula.

Using a serrated knife, trim off any uneven bits on the surface of the cooled cake.

Cut the cake in half, horizontally, and spread about 300 g (10½ oz) of the smooth salted caramel cream onto the bottom half leaving a 5 mm (¼ in) gap from the edge of the cake.

Place the top sponge, trimmed side down, on the caramel and press down gently. Dust with cocoa powder.

DARK CHOCOLATE
AND NUT BROWNIE

Serves 10–12

5 eggs
300 g (10½ oz) caster (superfine)
    sugar
400 g (14 oz) dark chocolate,
    roughly chopped
250 g (9 oz) unsalted butter
75 g (2¾ oz/½ cup) plain (all-
    purpose) flour
25 g (1 oz/¼ cup) Dutch
    (unsweetened) cocoa powder,
    plus extra for dusting
pinch of salt
150 g (5½ oz) toasted hazelnuts,
    roughly chopped
150 g (5½ oz) toasted almonds,
    roughly chopped
120 g (4½ oz) toasted pistachio
    nuts, roughly chopped
100 g (3½ oz) milk chocolate,
    roughly chopped
ice cream to serve (optional)
Hot chocolate sauce (see
    page 250) to serve (optional)

I had to put a brownie recipe in this book – it might be simple, but a moist, fresh brownie really is one of my favourite things. It's great on its own or as a component of a dessert. Store it in the freezer and slice from frozen as you need. It only takes a short while to defrost but I love frozen brownie as well as fresh and warm. Don't feel limited by the suggestions for inclusions. As long as you try to keep the same volume or quantity of nuts, you can try other types of nuts or even dried fruit, as you like. The inclusion of chocolate pieces in the batter takes this to the next level of chocolatey goodness.

Preheat the oven to 165°C (330°F). Spray a 28 x 13 x 6.5 cm (11 x 5 x 2½ in) loaf (bar) tin with canola oil and line with a strip of baking paper to cover the length of the tin plus overlap of a couple of centimetres (about an inch) either side. Spray the paper with oil.

Whisk the eggs and sugar in a freestanding electric mixer on medium speed for 10 minutes or until the mixture is thick and has doubled in volume. Reduce the speed to low and continue to mix.

Place 300 g (10½ oz) of the dark chocolate and all the butter in a bowl and melt together either in a microwave or over a double boiler.

Sift the flour, cocoa powder and salt into the chocolate mixture and mix well with a spatula. Add this mixture to the egg mixture in the electric mixer, with the mixer running on low. Mix well for 30 seconds. Remove the bowl from the machine and fold in the nuts, remaining chopped dark chocolate and the milk chocolate, using a rubber spatula.

Pour the mixture into the prepared tin and gently tap to level. Bake for 45 minutes or until a light crust has formed on top. The brownie needs to be underbaked to ensure its fudginess. It should still be a bit gooey when tested with a skewer.

Remove the pan from the oven and allow the brownie to cool in the tin for 20 minutes before turning it out onto a wire rack to cool completely.

Wrap in plastic wrap while still warm to keep the brownie moist, and store in the refrigerator overnight, or serve immediately. Slice and dust it with cocoa powder and serve with ice cream and chocolate sauce, if desired.

COCONUT RASPBERRY SPONGE WITH WHITE CHOCOLATE AND VANILLA MOUSSE

Serves 8–10

COMPONENTS
> Coconut raspberry sponge
> White chocolate and vanilla mousse
> White chocolate and vanilla glaze
> Raspberry jelly

This looks hard but it's not, I promise. Give it a go and watch your guests' envious looks as you effortlessly present this at the end of a meal. The sponge is easy to make and has the added bonus of being gluten-free so it really will suit everyone. Plan this and time it so you are glazing the cake as your guests arrive. It will look amazing and will be the perfect temperature by the time you're ready for dessert. This is a great cake to make for someone special, and is a fantastic way to finish a memorable meal.

COCONUT RASPBERRY SPONGE

50 g (1¾ oz) unsalted butter
60 g (2 oz) caster (superfine) sugar
2 eggs
90 g (3 oz) white chocolate, melted
80 g (2¾ oz) desiccated coconut
5 or 6 fresh or frozen raspberries

Preheat the oven to 160°C (320°F). Lightly spray canola oil into a round 18 cm (7 in) diameter x 4.5 cm (1¾ in) deep non-stick cake tin with a removable base. Cut an 18 cm (7 in) disc of baking paper and place it in the base of the tin.

Beat together the butter and the sugar using an electric mixer, or do it by hand. Add the eggs, one at a time, beating well after each addition.

Fold in the melted chocolate and then the coconut.

Pour the batter into the lined cake tin, or a metal pastry ring set on a baking tray lined with baking paper. Smooth the batter with a small palette knife or the back of a spoon then push in the raspberries, evenly spaced apart.

Bake for 30 minutes or until the sponge is cooked and is light and golden. Remove from the oven and leave the sponge to cool in the tin for 10–15 minutes before gently turning it out onto a chopping board. Chill in the refrigerator for 20 minutes.

Carefully peel the baking paper off the cake and cut a 15–16 cm (6–6¼ in) disc from the sponge. Discard (or eat) the trim. >

WHITE CHOCOLATE AND VANILLA MOUSSE

200 g (7 oz) white chocolate,
  roughly chopped
1 vanilla bean, seeds scraped
20 g (¾ oz) caster (superfine) sugar
3 gold-strength gelatine leaves
  (6 g/¼ oz) , soaked and drained
  (see page 33)
20 g (¾ oz) unsalted butter,
  at room temperature
280 ml (9½ fl oz) thickened
  (whipping) cream

Melt the white chocolate in a bowl in the microwave (see page 141).

Mix the vanilla seeds into the sugar and place in a saucepan with 120 ml (4 fl oz) water over medium heat. Stir and bring to the boil then remove the pan from the heat.

Add the gelatine to the pan, stir to dissolve it then strain the mixture over the melted chocolate. Add the butter and mix gently from the centre of the bowl to the outside of the bowl, using a spatula, until you have a smooth and shiny cream.

Whisk the cream to soft ribbons then fold this gently into the mousse base until you have a light and smooth mousse texture.

WHITE CHOCOLATE AND VANILLA GLAZE

300 g (10½ oz) white chocolate,
  chopped
125 ml (4 fl oz/½ cup) full-cream
  (whole) milk
1 vanilla bean, seeds scraped
25 ml (1 fl oz) liquid glucose
2 gold-strength gelatine leaves
  (4 g/⅕ oz), soaked and drained
  (see page 33)

Put the white chocolate in a bowl.

Bring the milk, vanilla seeds and glucose to the boil in a saucepan over medium heat then remove the pan from the heat.

Add the gelatine to the pan, stir to dissolve it then strain the mixture over the chocolate. Stir to combine.

Strain the glaze through a sieve and use it immediately or store in the refrigerator until ready to use.

Before using, simply reheat the glaze in short bursts on High (100%) in the microwave until it is warm and evenly heated (see page 60).

RASPBERRY JELLY

175 ml (6 fl oz) raspberry purée
  or juice
75 ml (2½ fl oz) Sugar syrup
  (see page 13)
1 g (¹⁄₁₆ oz) agar agar (see pages
  34–5)
3½ gold-strength gelatine leaves
  (7 g/¼ oz), soaked and drained
  (see page 33)

Place the purée, sugar syrup and agar agar in a small saucepan over medium heat, mix well and bring to the boil. Remove the pan from the heat.

Add the gelatine to the pan and stir to dissolve it. Pour the jelly into a lightly greased 1 litre (34 fl oz/4 cup) square or rectangular plastic container and leave the jelly to set in the refrigerator for 1 hour.

Turn the jelly out of the container onto a chopping board and cut out a 6 x 2 x 1 cm (2½ x ¾ x ½ in) piece of jelly with a sharp knife.

ASSEMBLY

1 tablespoon raspberry jam (see the recipe on page 52 if you would like to make your own)

white chocolate flakes (see page 143) (optional)

shaved fresh coconut (optional)

fresh raspberries, halved (optional)

Take an 18 cm (7 in) ring or cake tin, at least 5 cm (2 in) in height. Line the inside edges with baking paper strips cut to size and line the base with baking paper.

Take the sponge and invert it in the centre of the tin.

Spread a small quantity of raspberry jam onto the sponge using a small palette knife or the back of a spoon.

Pour the white chocolate and vanilla mousse on top of the sponge and gently tap the tray to level the mousse flat. Use a palette knife to make sure it's really flat and again tap to level it off as best you can.

Place the cake tin in the freezer to set for a minimum of 4 hours – it's essential the cake is frozen before you glaze it.

Unmould the frozen cake and remove the paper from the base. Place it on a wire rack over a tray and glaze the cake, following the instructions on page 61.

Gently tap the rack to remove any excess glaze and lift the cake onto a serving plate with a palette knife.

Allow the cake to thaw for at least 45 minutes before finishing with the jelly and garnishing with the chocolate flakes, coconut shavings and fresh raspberries, if desired.

> TIP: Make the cake, glaze and jelly the day before serving for convenience. Glaze the cake a couple of hours before serving.

Sweet Essentials

JELLIES

Jellies are fun and simple to make and add an extra texture to desserts and cakes. There are several ways to make jellies and there are so many ingredients you can use to 'set' them. Here I will show you two of those ingredients – gelatine and agar agar, which are the most common. They can be used alone or combined. Once you realise how easy they are to use you'll be making jellies all the time.

GELATINE

This is the most common ingredient used to set jellies and it comes in leaf or powdered form. Powdered gelatine is something I don't use as I feel the texture is not as good as leaves, and I believe there is a stronger flavour present, which I'm not keen on. The leaves (also called sheets) come in different strengths, known as 'bloom'.

I use gold-strength gelatine in everything and I recommend you do too for the best results with the recipes in this book. It's easy to use and widely available online. You can also find it in specialist delicatessens and cooking shops and it is also starting to appear in the baking section of supermarkets.

Gelatine-based jellies can be set, melted and reset, which makes them quite versatile as well as easy to use. They melt between 27°C (81°F) and 40°C (104°F), which is great because it means they will melt in the mouth, giving a real burst of flavour.

Gelatine is produced from animals and is therefore not suitable for vegetarians and vegans. Instead, you could use agar agar, which is derived from seaweed (see page 34).

How to use gelatine leaves

Gelatine leaves need to be softened before use and this is easy to do. Simply weigh the correct quantity of gelatine for your recipe. Pull the leaves apart and soak them in a bowl of cold water for a few minutes to soften. Remove the softened leaves from the water and gently squeeze out the excess water and discard it. Dissolve or melt the leaves in a warm liquid. Don't whisk the jelly as you don't want bubbles, but stir the jelly gently to dissolve the gelatine and then strain the mixture through a sieve.

HOW TO USE GELATINE LEAVES

1 Weigh the gelatine leaves then pull them apart and then soak the leaves in cold water.

2 Submerge each leaf individually in the water to ensure the gelatine does not clump together.

3 After a couple of minutes remove the now-softened gelatine leaves from the water and gently squeeze out and discard the soaking liquid.

4 Add the gelatine to your chosen heated liquid and stir in well to dissolve, using a spoon. Do not whisk.

5 Strain the jelly mixture into a bowl or mould. Leave to set in the refrigerator for at least 2 hours.

6 Your set jelly is now ready to be spooned onto your dish (see page 35) or to unmould.

LIQUIDS TO USE FOR JELLY

As well as water, you can use fruit purées, juice, tea or coffee and flavoured waters to make a jelly. Pretty much most liquids will set including milk-based ones (such as for panna cotta). You may have trouble setting anything too sweet and syrupy, so add water to get a nice balanced mix and then set your jelly.

JELLY RECIPE USING GELATINE
Makes 500 ml (17 fl oz/2 cups)

500 ml (17 fl oz/2 cups) liquid
4 gold-strength gelatine leaves (8 g/¼ oz), soaked and
  drained (see page 33)

Place 300 ml (10 fl oz) of the liquid in a saucepan over medium–low heat and bring to a simmer. Remove from the heat and add the gelatine. Stir gently to dissolve it then add the remaining cold liquid to the mixture and stir. Strain the liquid through a fine sieve into serving dishes or glasses. Leave the mixture to set in the refrigerator for a minimum of 2 hours.

AGAR AGAR

This is a little less popular as a gelling agent, and has a more textural/brittle mouthfeel to it than gelatine. It can be found fairly easily in Asian supermarkets or online. Agar agar is derived from seaweed so it is perfect for vegetarian and vegan diets. It activates when heated and sets quickly. It is stronger than gelatine, which means it cuts really cleanly with a sharp knife and melts at a much higher temperature, so you can handle it for longer. I tend to use agar agar and gelatine together in some of my jellies as I like the wobbly, clear and pleasant mouthfeel qualities of gelatine with the strength and ease-of-use benefits of agar agar (see opposite).

How to use agar agar

Agar agar comes in powdered form and dissolves in a cold or warm liquid. Just weigh the required quantity and whisk it into the liquid. Heat the liquid to the boil, while stirring constantly with a silicone spatula, to activate the jelly. Then pour the mixture into a container and leave it to set. You can then cut the jelly with a sharp knife or even pastry cutters.

JELLY RECIPE USING GELATINE AND AGAR AGAR

1 Sprinkle the agar agar into the cool liquid and soak the gelatine in cold water. Heat the agar agar to the boil, remove from the heat and stir in the soaked gelatine.

2 Strain the jelly mixture into a jug and pour it onto a lightly greased, shallow surface to a thickness of a couple of millimetres (⅛ in).

3 Leave the jelly to set in the refrigerator for at least 30 minutes. Use a small sharp knife to cut the jelly into the desired shape. Gently lift the jelly using a small palette knife.

JELLY RECIPE USING AGAR AGAR
Makes 500 ml (17 fl oz/2 cups)

5 g (¼ oz) agar agar
500 ml (17 fl oz/2 cups) liquid

Whisk the agar agar into the liquid and place the mixture in a saucepan over medium heat. Cook, stirring constantly, until it boils. Remove from the heat and pour the mixture into a lightly greased plastic container or shallow tray to set.

GELATINE AND AGAR AGAR TOGETHER MAKE A GREAT JELLY

This is my most used recipe for jelly. It is super-easy to make and is very versatile. Make the jelly and pour the mixture into small silicone moulds and leave to set in the freezer. The moulded jelly will pop out easily and can be used to garnish cakes and desserts. Alternatively, pour the mixture onto a flat or patterned, shallow tray lightly greased with canola spray. The jelly will set quickly. Harden it in the refrigerator for 1 hour then cut it into shapes using a knife or pastry cutters.

JELLY RECIPE USING GELATINE AND AGAR AGAR
Makes 500 ml (17 fl oz/2 cups)

2.5 g (⅛ oz) agar agar
500 ml (17 fl oz/2 cups) liquid
6 gold-strength gelatine leaves (12 g/¼ oz), soaked and drained (see page 33)

Whisk the agar agar into the liquid in a saucepan then place over medium heat. Cook, stirring constantly, until it boils. Remove from the heat and stir in the soaked gelatine. Pour the mixture into moulds, containers or trays. (See the step-by-step instructions opposite.)

SPOONING OUT JELLY

A lovely way of serving small pieces of jelly on or in a dessert is by setting your jelly in a plastic container and scooping it out with a spoon. Boil water in a kettle and pour some water into a mug. Place a spoon in the mug for a few seconds and then dry it off with a tea towel (dish towel). Use a hot spoon to 'scoop' some of the jelly from the container and place it on your dessert. The heat of the spoon will leave a 'shine' on the gelatine. (See the step-by-step instructions below.)

SPOONING OUT JELLY

1 Place your spoon in boiling water to heat it up before you start to spoon.

2 Use the hot spoon to scoop some of the jelly onto your dessert or cake.

3 Using the hot spoon will give your pieces of jelly a lovely shine.

LAMINGTONS

Makes 9

COMPONENTS
> My lamington sponge
> Dark chocolate covering

I absolutely love lamingtons and so does my wife, Cath – they are her favourite. I make batches of these and they freeze really well. We also like to eat them frozen, but maybe that's just us? Anyway, these lamingtons are a fantastic version of this popular cake. The jam is the best part and the cavity-filling method is a neat trick. The sponge is delicious and can be used as a Madeira sponge as well if you like.

MY LAMINGTON SPONGE

8 eggs, at room temperature
finely grated zest of ½ lemon
2 vanilla beans, seeds scraped
275 g (9½ oz) caster (superfine)
   sugar
275 g (9½ oz) self-raising flour
1 teaspoon baking powder
200 g (7 oz) unsalted butter, melted
raspberry jam as needed (see the
   recipe on page 52 if you would like
   to make your own)

Preheat the oven to 180°C (350°F). Grease a 20 x 20 x 6 cm (8 x 8 x 2½ in) square non-stick cake tin. Line the base and sides with baking paper cut to size.

Using an electric mixer, whisk the eggs, lemon zest, vanilla seeds and sugar on medium–high speed for 20 minutes. The mixture should be thick and pale.

Sift the flour with the baking powder, then gently fold this into the egg mixture using a spatula.

Take around 200 g (7 oz) of the batter and whisk it into the cooled, melted – but still liquid – butter and then transfer this mixture back to the bowl with the remaining batter. Fold all together well but gently, using a spatula or metal spoon.

Bake in the oven for 25–30 minutes until cooked through. A skewer inserted into the centre of the sponge should come out clean. Remove from the oven and leave the sponge to cool in the tin completely.

Remove the sponge from the tin and trim any brown edges off with a serrated knife. You should be left with a clean, square sponge with the approximate dimensions of 18 x 18 x 5 cm (7 x 7 x 2 in).

Use a sharp knife to cut the sponge into nine 5 cm (2 in) cubes. Freeze any trimmed sponge to fold into ice cream another time.

Take a melon baller and scoop out two balls from the sponge. Fill the cavity with raspberry jam from a piping (icing) bag and plug the hole with the first scooped sponge ball. Fill all nine sponge cubes and place them, covered with plastic wrap, in the refrigerator for 1 hour to harden slightly before covering with chocolate.

DARK CHOCOLATE COVERING

600 g (1 lb 5 oz) dark chocolate, roughly chopped
200 ml (7 fl oz) thickened (whipping) cream
200 ml (7 fl oz) full-cream (whole) milk

Melt the chocolate in the microwave (see page 141).

Heat the cream and milk together in a saucepan over medium heat until it starts to boil. Pour the hot milk mixture over the chocolate and stir to emulsify until you have a smooth, shiny cream.

ASSEMBLY

600 g (1 lb 5 oz) desiccated coconut

Scatter some of the desiccated coconut onto a shallow baking tray.

Remove the sponges from the refrigerator and use two forks or skewers to dip the sponges in the chocolate covering. Gently shake off any excess chocolate and immediately place the dipped sponge in the tray of coconut. Sprinkle over some of the remaining coconut and ensure the lamingtons are covered entirely before placing them on a wire rack over a tray to set for 30 minutes before scoffing.

See photograph on the following page.

Left: Glamingtons (page 40);
right: Lamingtons (page 36).

GLAMINGTONS

Makes 9

COMPONENTS
> Raspberry sorbet
> Malibu syrup
> White chocolate lamington sponge
> Dark chocolate covering

Whaaaaat? Just when you thought a lamington couldn't get any more fabulous… These glamour cakes are the best dressed at any VIP event. The gold adds a luxurious touch and the Malibu syrup takes it to the next level. Roll out the red carpet – head back and smile for the camera.

RASPBERRY SORBET

65 g (2¼ oz) caster (superfine) sugar
250 ml (8½ fl oz/1 cup) raspberry
   purée
1 teaspoon liquid glucose
squeeze of lemon juice

Place 40 ml (1¼ fl oz) water and the sugar in a small saucepan over medium heat and bring to the boil. Stir to dissolve the sugar then remove from the heat. Stir in the remaining ingredients and leave to cool in the refrigerator. Churn in an ice cream maker according to the manufacturer's instructions then store in the freezer until required.

MALIBU SYRUP

90 g (3 oz) caster (superfine) sugar
200 ml (7 fl oz) Malibu

Place 200 ml (7 fl oz) water and the sugar in a small saucepan over medium heat and bring to the boil. Stir to dissolve the sugar then remove the pan from the heat. Stir in the Malibu. Set aside.

WHITE CHOCOLATE LAMINGTON SPONGE

6 egg whites
70 g (2½ oz) caster (superfine) sugar
6 egg yolks
35 g (1¼ oz) icing (confectioners')
   sugar
1 vanilla bean, seeds scraped
95 g (3¼ oz) butter, at room
   temperature
200 g (7 oz) white chocolate, melted
200 g (7 oz/1⅓ cups) plain
   (all-purpose) flour, sifted
1 teaspoon salt
70 g (2½ oz) desiccated coconut

Preheat the oven to 180°C (350°F). Grease a 20 x 20 x 6 cm (8 x 8 x 2½ in) square non-stick cake tin. Line the base and sides with baking paper cut to size.

Whisk the egg whites in a freestanding electric mixer on medium–high speed and gradually add the caster sugar to form a glossy meringue. Transfer the meringue to a larger bowl.

Wash the bowl and use the electric mixer fitted with the paddle attachment. Beat the egg yolks, icing sugar and vanilla seeds on medium–high speed for 10 minutes. The mixture will become pale and frothy. At this point, with the mixer running, add the butter and mix in well before adding the melted white chocolate.

Remove the bowl from the mixer and fold in half the meringue mixture. Then gently fold in the sifted flour, salt and coconut.

Transfer the mixture to the larger bowl with the remaining egg white and fold it in gently.

Pour the mixture into the prepared tin and bake for 25 minutes or until golden brown. Remove from the oven and leave to cool in the tin until cool enough to turn out. Leave to cool completely on a wire rack before trimming the top, bottom and sides of the sponge and cutting it into nine 5 cm (2 in) cubes.

Take an apple corer and cut an incision into the side of each sponge halfway through. Fill the cavity with raspberry jam from a piping (icing) bag and plug the hole with the cored sponge. Fill all nine sponge cubes and then dab each side of the sponges with some of the Malibu syrup using a pastry brush.

Place the sponges, covered, in the refrigerator for 1 hour to harden slightly, before covering with chocolate.

DARK CHOCOLATE COVERING

600 g (1 lb 5 oz) dark chocolate, roughly chopped
200 ml (7 fl oz) thickened (whipping) cream
200 ml (7 fl oz) full-cream (whole) milk

Melt the chocolate in the microwave (see page 141).

Heat the cream and milk together in a saucepan over medium heat until it starts to boil then pour it over the chocolate. Stir to emulsify until you have a smooth, shiny cream.

ASSEMBLY

edible gold lustre as needed
400 g (14 oz) shredded coconut
100 g (3½ oz) white chocolate shavings (see pages 142–3) brushed with edible gold lustre, if desired

Mix the gold lustre with the coconut and chocolate and pour this mixture into a shallow tray.

Remove the sponges from the refrigerator and use two forks or skewers to dip the lamington sponges in the chocolate covering. Gently shake off any excess chocolate and place the dipped sponge in the tray of gold and coconut.

Roll the lamingtons entirely in the coconut and place them on a wire rack (over a tray) to set for 20 minutes before transferring them to a plate and serving with the raspberry sorbet.

See photograph on pages 38–39.

SPICED APPLE CAKE WITH THICK VANILLA CUSTARD

Serves 6–8

COMPONENTS
> Spiced push-in pastry
> Apple filling
> Thick vanilla custard

My wife, Cath, gave me this recipe, which I am grateful for. She comes from the Victorian country town of Bacchus Marsh. The town is renowned for its fertile soil that yields plenty of quality fruit and veggies – in particular, apples. Her mum, Trish, made this for Cath when she was growing up and it reminds me of the apple desserts that my mum made for me too. Certainly some of the best food stems from our childhood memories. Everybody who tries this cake loves it! Cath has reworked the recipe a little, so thanks to Trish and Cath for sharing this with me, and now you guys.

SPICED PUSH-IN PASTRY

120 g (4½ oz) unsalted butter, softened
110 g (4 oz) caster (superfine) sugar
pinch of salt
1 egg
250 g (9 oz/1⅔ cups) self-raising flour
1 teaspoon mixed allspice
1 teaspoon ground ginger
1 teaspoon ground cinnamon

Cream the butter, sugar and salt together on medium speed in a freestanding electric mixer fitted with the paddle attachment. Add the egg and mix well before incorporating the sifted flour and spices.

Wrap the pastry in plastic wrap and leave to rest for about 20 minutes in the refrigerator, or until required.

APPLE FILLING

12 (approximately 1.2 kg/2 lb 10 oz) pink lady apples
1 vanilla bean, seeds scraped
finely grated zest and juice of 1 lemon
150 g (5½ oz) caster (superfine) sugar

Peel the apples, cut them into quarters and remove the core. Cut each quarter into four pieces.

Place the apples, vanilla seeds and pod, lemon zest and juice and sugar in a large microwave-safe dish with a lid that allows the steam to escape.

Cook on High (100%) in the microwave for 20–25 minutes, stirring every 5 minutes to ensure even cooking.

The apples are ready when they are soft but whole. Discard the vanilla pods. Leave the apples to cool completely before assembling the cake. >

THICK VANILLA CUSTARD

275 ml (9½ fl oz) thickened
    (whipping) cream
275 ml (9½ fl oz) full-cream
    (whole) milk
1 vanilla bean, seeds scraped
95 g (3¼ oz) caster (superfine) sugar
20 g (¾ oz) cornflour (cornstarch)
3 egg yolks

Combine the cream, milk and vanilla seeds and pod in a saucepan over medium heat and bring to a simmer. Remove the pan from the heat and discard the vanilla pod.

Whisk the sugar, cornflour and egg yolks together well until the mixture is pale and thick.

Pour one-third of the hot milk mixture into the egg and sugar mixture and whisk well to combine.

Pour this mixture back into the saucepan with the remaining milk/cream and mix well with a spatula or wooden spoon.

Place the pan back over medium–low heat and whisk constantly while cooking the custard until it starts to boil and bubbles start to break the surface. Cook at this temperature for a further 20 seconds, stirring constantly.

Serve immediately or transfer the custard to the bowl of a freestanding electric mixer fitted with the paddle attachment. Mix the custard on a low to medium speed until it cools to room temperature. Store the custard in the refrigerator until needed.

ASSEMBLY

1 egg yolk
splash of full-cream (whole) milk
golden caster (superfine) sugar for
    sprinkling

Preheat the oven to 165°C (330°F). Lightly grease a 22.5 cm (9 in) round and 5–6 cm (2–2½ in) deep non-stick springform cake tin.

Take about two-thirds of the pastry and knead it on a lightly dusted work surface. Roll the pastry to 5 mm (¼ in) thick and line the tin. (See page 81–2 for more instructions.) The pastry is very fragile but easy to fix. You can roll it onto baking paper and chill it before pressing it into the tin with your fingers. Don't worry if there are holes or you think you are making a mess; just use your fingers to push in the pastry.

Line the pastry up the side of the tin and then add the cooled apple filling. Pack the apple in nice and tight.

Roll out the remaining pastry to the same thickness as the base and use it to create the pie lid. Press the edges together with your fingers to seal. Cut out apple shapes from any remaining pastry to decorate the top of the pie.

Lightly beat the egg yolk and milk and lightly brush this mixture onto the surface of the cake. Sprinkle with some golden caster sugar. Bake in the oven for 45–50 minutes, turning halfway through cooking.

Allow to cool in the tin for 10 minutes before removing. Serve immediately with the thick vanilla custard or some thickened (whipping) cream.

CHOCOLATE, PEAR
AND HAZELNUT CAKE

Serves 12–16

COMPONENTS
> Poached pears
> Chocolate, pear and hazelnut cake

This is a really fudgy and delicious cake that is suitable for gluten-free diets. This cake forms the base of one of my most popular mousse cakes at Sweet Studio but, as you can see here, it stands up really well on its own.

POACHED PEARS

150 g (5½ oz) caster (superfine)
   sugar
1 vanilla bean, seeds scraped
zest and juice of ½ lemon
2 pears, peeled and cored

Place the sugar, 500 ml (17 fl oz/2 cups) water, the scraped vanilla seeds and lemon zest and juice in a medium saucepan over medium heat and bring the mixture to the boil, stirring until the sugar has completely dissolved.

Add the peeled and cored pears and reduce the heat to low. Allow to simmer for approximately 10–15 minutes or until the pears are soft enough for you to easily insert a paring knife into the flesh.

Turn off the heat and allow the pears to cool in the syrup.

Once cool, slice each pear into four pieces lengthways.

> TIP: You can use tinned pears instead of poached pears. >

<

CHOCOLATE, PEAR AND HAZELNUT CAKE

225 g (8 oz) dark chocolate,
  roughly chopped
115 g (4 oz) unsalted butter
6 egg yolks, lightly beaten
90 g (3 oz) ground hazelnuts
90 g (3 oz/½ cup) rice flour
60 g (2 oz) hazelnuts, lightly toasted
6 egg whites
200 g (7 oz) caster (superfine)
  sugar

Preheat the oven to 170°C (340°F).

Grease a 22.5 cm (9 in) round non-stick springform cake tin.
Line the tin with baking paper on the base and side cut to size.

Melt the dark chocolate and butter together in the microwave. Melt
it on High (100%) in short 20-second bursts, stirring well in between
each burst.

Transfer the chocolate and butter mixture to a mixing bowl.

Stir in the egg yolks and mix well, followed by the ground hazelnuts
and the rice flour. Mix well again – the mixture will thicken and look
separated. Mix in the whole hazelnuts.

Whisk the egg whites using an electric mixer until you have a stiff
meringue then add the sugar in three batches. The meringue will
become a little wet. At this point fold it into the chocolate base in
two batches.

Pour the batter into the prepared tin and arrange the slices of pear on
top, going around in a circle like the hands of a clock.

Bake in the oven for 35–40 minutes or until just cooked. You want the
centre of the cake to still be a bit moist, as it will go fudgy once cooled.
A crust should have formed on top of the cake.

Remove the cake from the oven and allow it to cool in the tin before
turning it out.

TO SERVE

thickened (whipping) cream
  to serve (optional)

Once the cake has cooled, serve it immediately with thickened cream,
if desired.

PERFECT JAM SWISS ROLL

Serves 8

6 eggs, at room temperature
1 vanilla bean, seeds scraped
zest of ½ lemon
200 g (7 oz) caster (superfine)
   sugar, plus extra for sprinkling
130 g (4½ oz) plain (all-purpose)
   flour (or cake or soft flour if you
   can find it)
100 ml (3½ fl oz) thickened
   (whipping) cream
1 teaspoon icing (confectioners')
   sugar, plus extra for dusting
70 g (2½ oz) jam (I like raspberry –
   see the recipe on page 52 if you
   would like to make your own)

Preheat the oven to 190°C (375°F). Grease a 30 x 20 cm (12 x 8 in) baking tray with a 2 cm (¾ in) lip. Line the tray with sheet of baking paper, exactly the same size as the base. Spray the paper with some canola oil.

Place the eggs, half the vanilla seeds and the lemon zest in a freestanding electric mixer and start to whisk on medium–high speed.

Place the sugar on a sheet of baking paper on a separate baking tray and place in the oven for 2 minutes to heat it up. Pour the warm sugar into the bowl with the whisking eggs. Whisk on medium speed until the mixture has doubled and you can see thick ribbons in the mixture.

Sift the flour and fold it into the mixture using a metal spoon or spatula. Do this in three stages to maintain the aeration.

Spread the batter on the prepared tray using a palette knife, spreading it evenly to the edges of the tray. Bake for 8 minutes or until the sponge has cooked to an even colour. Remove the sponge from the oven and let it sit for a minute.

Place a sheet of baking paper (just larger than the size of the sponge) on a work surface. Turn the paper so it is oriented portrait and sprinkle some extra caster sugar over the entire surface. Turn the cooked sponge out onto the baking paper on the sugar and peel the baking paper off the sponge. (See pages 54–5 for step-by-step instructions.)

Take a sharp knife and score a line across the bottom of the sponge 2 cm (¾ in) from the bottom edge, but do not cut all the way through.

Roll the sponge while still warm, using the paper to help. Roll from bottom to top and roll the paper inside the sponge. Once rolled, leave the sponge to cool for 20 minutes at room temperature.

Whip the cream with the remaining vanilla seeds and the icing sugar to thick ribbons.

Unroll the sponge and remove the paper. Spread the jam evenly over the sponge, leaving a 2 cm (¾ in) gap at the end of the sponge where there was no incision. Add the cream and spread again leaving the same gap at the end.

Re-roll the sponge, leaving the paper out. Dust with icing sugar, trim the ends and serve with a cup of tea.

Sweet Essentials

MAKING YOUR OWN JAM

Homemade jam beats the store-bought stuff every time. You only need a couple of ingredients and little equipment – maybe a decent pan and a thermometer. Below I have included two of my favourite recipes, but feel free to use whatever fruit you wish as these recipes work with other fruits – try strawberry instead of raspberry and peach instead of apricot. You can buy jam-setting sugar from most supermarkets.

RASPBERRY JAM
Makes 750 g (1 lb 11 oz)

500 g (1 lb 2 oz) fresh or frozen raspberries
500 g (1 lb 2 oz) jam-setting sugar
juice of ½ lemon

Place the raspberries and sugar in a heavy-based saucepan over medium heat. I prefer a cast-iron pan as it keeps the heat and cooks the jam more quickly and evenly. Mash the fruit with a fork.

Heat the mixture, stirring frequently with a wooden spoon or heat-resistant spatula. Bring to the boil then place a sugar or digital thermometer in the pan. Continue to cook and stir, being careful as the jam is very hot and it may start to spit at you as you stir the mixture.

Cook the jam to a temperature of 103°C (217°F) using the thermometer to check and ensuring you continue to stir so the jam does not stick to the base of the pan.

Once the temperature has been reached, remove the pan from the heat and strain in the lemon juice. Stir then leave the jam to sit for 5 minutes to allow it to settle. Use a spoon to skim any scum from the surface. Ladle or pour the jam into sterilised jars and place a clean lid tightly on top.

Store in the refrigerator or pantry for up to a year.

APRICOT AND VANILLA JAM
Makes 750 g (1 lb 11 oz)

500 g (1 lb 2 oz) apricots, halved and stones removed
500 g (1 lb 2 oz) jam-setting sugar
2 vanilla beans, seeds scraped
juice of ½ lemon

Place the apricots, sugar and vanilla seeds in a bowl and blitz with a hand-held blender, or in a stand blender or food processor, to get rid of any big chunks of fruit. Transfer the mixture to a heavy-based saucepan over medium heat. I prefer a cast-iron pan as it keeps the heat and cooks the jam more quickly and evenly.

Heat the mixture, stirring frequently with a wooden spoon or heat-resistant spatula. Bring to the boil then place a sugar or digital thermometer in the pan. Continue to cook and stir, being careful as the jam is very hot and it may start to spit at you as you stir the mixture.

Cook the jam to a temperature of 103°C (217°F) using the thermometer to check and ensuring you continue to stir so the jam does not stick to the base of the pan.

Once the temperature has been reached, remove the pan from the heat and strain in the lemon juice. Stir then leave the jam to sit for 5 minutes to allow it to settle. Use a spoon to skim any scum from the surface. Ladle or pour the jam into sterilised jars and place a clean lid tightly on top.

Store in the refrigerator or pantry for up to a year.

Raspberry jam

Sweet Essentials

ASSEMBLING A SWISS ROLL

When I taste a Swiss roll (jelly roll) it really reminds me of my childhood and of a time without the stress and frantic pace of today. Simpler times called for simpler food, especially with cakes and desserts, but that doesn't mean they lacked in pleasure. Perhaps it is nostalgia but a well-made Swiss roll with lots of jam and cream has to be one of the joys of life.

Swiss rolls are easy to make as well, especially when you follow these step-by-step assembly instructions for the recipe on page 51. The sponge itself is pretty simple; just ensure that it is baked correctly. The sponge should not be under-baked or, indeed, over-baked, otherwise rolling will be a sticky or crumbly mess.

It always helps to have a visual on the finishing and rolling. Follow the tips on the opposite page and you will achieve victory rolls time and time again, just like Nichole, my Swiss roll model on page 50.

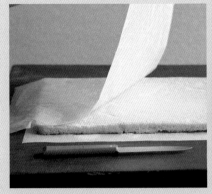  

1 Lay a sheet of baking paper (just larger than the sponge) on a work surface. Sprinkle caster (superfine) sugar over the top. Turn the cooked sponge out onto the sugared paper and remove the paper it was cooked on.

2 Using a sharp knife, score a line across the bottom of the sponge 2 cm (¾ in) from the bottom edge, but do not cut all the way through.

3 Roll up the sponge while it is still warm, with the sheet of sugared baking paper inside it. Roll from bottom to top.

4 Once rolled, leave to cool for 20 minutes. Prepare the cream and jam filling for the Swiss roll.

5 Unroll the sponge and lay it flat again. Place the jam on the sponge.

6 Spread the jam evenly over the sponge, leaving a 2 cm (¾ in) gap at the unscored end.

7 Add the cream and spread it over the sponge, again leaving the gap at the unscored end.

8 Starting from the incision end, leaving the paper out, roll up the sponge.

9 When the sponge is rolled, dust with icing (confectioners') sugar, trim the ends and serve.

ULTIMATE CHOCOLATE AND HAZELNUT BIRTHDAY CAKE

Serves 6–8

COMPONENTS
> Chocolate and hazelnut sponge
> Orange syrup
> Milk chocolate cream
> Dark chocolate cream
> Dark chocolate glaze

This is a cake that will be remembered for years to come – hopefully it will become your family's favourite birthday cake. It delivers in both taste and presentation. After glazing you can finish the cake as you please. I've kept the exterior simple but you can go nuts.

All of the component recipes are bang on in their own right and can be used independently, but together they make something very special.

CHOCOLATE AND HAZELNUT SPONGE

4 eggs, at room temperature
4 egg yolks, at room temperature
1 tablespoon liquid glucose
4 egg whites, at room temperature
30 g (1 oz) caster (superfine) sugar
150 g (5½ oz) icing (confectioners') sugar
40 g (1½ oz) plain (all-purpose) flour
40 g (1½ oz/⅓ cup) cornflour (cornstarch)
80 g (2¾ oz) Dutch (unsweetened) cocoa powder
160 g (5½ oz) ground hazelnuts
pinch of salt

Preheat the oven to 180°C (350°F). Grease and line the base of a 22.5 cm (9 in) non-stick springform cake tin with canola oil and baking paper.

Place the eggs, yolks and liquid glucose in the bowl of a freestanding electric mixer and whisk on medium speed for 15 minutes or until thick. Transfer the mixture to another larger bowl.

Wash and dry the mixer bowl and add the egg whites. Whisk on medium speed until frothy, then gradually add the caster sugar and whisk to a stiff meringue. Fold this gently into the egg yolk mixture.

Sift the icing sugar, plain flour, cornflour and cocoa powder into a bowl and add the hazelnuts and salt. Gently fold this into the eggs using a spatula until all is incorporated.

Pour the mixture into the prepared cake tin and bake for 25 minutes or until cooked. A skewer inserted into the centre of the cake should come out clean.

Remove from the oven and leave to cool in the tin for 5 minutes. Run a small knife around the inside edge to loosen the cake from the tin. Remove the cake from the tin and allow it to cool for 40 minutes on a wire rack.

ORANGE SYRUP

150 g (5½ oz) caster (superfine)
  sugar
finely grated zest of 1 orange

Place 200 ml (7 fl oz) water with the sugar and orange zest in a saucepan over medium–low heat. Bring to a gentle simmer and stir to ensure the sugar has dissolved before removing the pan from the heat.

MILK CHOCOLATE CREAM

350 g (12½ oz) milk chocolate,
  roughly chopped
550 ml (18½ fl oz) thickened
  (whipping) cream

Put the chocolate in a bowl.

Heat 200 ml (7 fl oz) of the cream in a saucepan over medium heat until it starts to boil. Pour the hot cream over the chocolate. Leave to sit for 20 seconds before stirring to emulsify the chocolate.

Add the remaining cream and again mix well. Store the cream in the refrigerator for a minimum of 2 hours.

DARK CHOCOLATE CREAM

340 g (12 oz) dark chocolate,
  roughly chopped
125 g (4½ oz) unsalted butter,
  softened
375 ml (12½ fl oz/1½ cups)
  thickened (whipping) cream
1 tablespoon liquid glucose

Put the chocolate and butter in a bowl.

Place the cream and glucose in a saucepan over medium heat and bring to the boil. Remove from the heat and pour over the chocolate and butter. Leave to sit for 20 seconds before stirring to emulsify the chocolate into a smooth, shiny cream. Leave to cool at room temperature until thick enough to spread with a palette knife.

DARK CHOCOLATE GLAZE

180 g (6½ oz) caster (superfine)
  sugar
60 g (2 oz) Dutch (unsweetened)
  cocoa powder
100 ml (3½ fl oz) thickened
  (whipping) cream
5 gold-strength gelatine leaves
  (10 g/¼ oz), soaked and drained
  (see page 33)

Place the sugar in a large bowl and sift in the cocoa powder to ensure any lumps are removed. Add 140 ml (4½ fl oz) water, stirring to make a paste. Put this paste with the cream in a large heavy-based saucepan over medium heat. Stirring constantly, bring the mixture to the boil. Stir and boil for 1 minute before removing from the heat. Add the gelatine to the pan, stirring until it is dissolved.

Strain the glaze through a fine sieve into a jug and leave to cool. Bubbles may appear on the surface of the glaze. Wait until the glaze has cooled down before skimming the surface well with a spoon. Store the glaze in covered plastic containers in the refrigerator until ready to use. >

ASSEMBLY

apricot or rasberry jam (see the
recipes on page 52 if you'd like to
make your own)
White chocolate shavings (see
pages 142–3) to garnish

Cut the sponge into three layers horizontally, using a serrated knife.

The top piece will be the base so invert it with the exposed baked piece side down, onto a cake board. The inverted base of the cake will be used for the top, as it is flat. The other piece of sponge, cut on both sides, will be in the middle.

Reheat the orange syrup and dab it onto the sponge pieces using a pastry brush, to moisten each layer on both sides.

Spread the jam liberally on the bottom layer and middle layer sponges.

Place the milk chocolate cream in a freestanding electric mixer and whisk on medium–high speed to a thick consistency.

Spread about 120 g (4½ oz) of the milk chocolate cream onto the jam on the bottom layer of sponge. Spoon the cream into the middle and push with a spatula to the edges of the sponge leaving a gap of 1 cm (½ in) around the edge.

Place the middle sponge on top of the milk chocolate cream ensuring the jam is facing upwards. Repeat the milk chocolate cream step and place the top layer of sponge on top of the cream. Push down gently to flatten it evenly.

Place the cake in the refrigerator for a minimum of 2 hours to set.

Remove the cake from the refrigerator and, using a spatula or palette knife, smear and smooth the dark chocolate cream over the top and side of the cake. Be fairly generous with the cream using around two-thirds of the total amount and try to smooth the side as best you can.

Place the cake back in the refrigerator for an hour to set. Remove from the refrigerator and repeat with the remaining dark chocolate cream. Place the cake back in the refrigerator.

Melt the dark chocolate glaze in the microwave (see page 60), stirring gently, until it is liquid again. Do not use a whisk, as you do not want air bubbles. Ensure the glaze is heated evenly before setting it aside to cool. Use a sugar or digital thermometer to check the temperature of the glaze. If the glaze is too hot it will melt the cake but too cold will not be neat. When the glaze reaches a temperature of 40°C (104°F) it is ready to use. Use a sugar or digital thermometer for accuracy.

Glaze the cake following the instructions on page 61, and remove any drips.

Place the cake on a serving plate or cake stand. Finish the cake with a few white chocolate shavings then serve.

Sweet Essentials

GLAZING

Glazing is a great skill for you to acquire and will make your cakes and desserts look really professional. It's super-easy to do and I always make batches of glaze and store them in the refrigerator in plastic containers until needed. I then reheat the glaze gently in a microwave and glaze my cakes from frozen. The cold temperature of the cake will help to set the gelatine-based glaze and the fluidity of the glaze will ensure a flat and even finish.

GLAZE RECIPES

There are two glaze recipes in this book, one being a chocolate (cocoa powder) based glaze (see photograph below right and recipe page 57) and the other a milk-based white glaze with vanilla (see photograph above right and recipe page 30). The white one can be coloured if you wish by adding a water-soluble colour to the glaze when you mix in the chocolate. However, make sure you strain the glaze after any addition of colouring agent.

Both these glaze recipes can be used for other cakes and desserts. I find both of them are extremely useful additions to the sweet kitchen.

REHEATING GLAZES BEFORE USE

When reheating glazes, I like to do so in short and high bursts in the microwave. I heat for 30 seconds on High (100%) and stir the glaze with a spoon, then heat again. I like to bring the glaze to a fairly high temperature of around 60–70°C (140–158°F), which will make the glaze become nice and shiny. I then leave the glaze at room temperature, stirring intermittently, until the temperature drops to 35–40°C (95–104°F) before glazing the cake. I use a digital thermometer to check the temperature accurately. If you use a glaze that is too hot it can melt the cake and run off quickly, leaving a very thin finish.

After reheating a glaze, leave it at room temperature to cool, stirring occasionally, until the temperature drops to 35–40°C (95–104°F) before use. Use a digital thermometer to check the temperature accurately.

GLAZING A CAKE

Remove your cake from the freezer once your glaze is at the correct temperature. Set the cake on a wire rack placed over a shallow tray. Pour the glaze onto the centre of the cake in one motion and try to ensure the glaze runs evenly over the top of the cake and runs to cover the entire surface of the cake and down the side. Then leave the glaze to stop dripping and set before trimming the bottom of the cake with a small palette knife. Lift the cake using two palette knives and place it on a serving plate or cake stand. Finish the cake as you wish and leave at room temperature for 30–40 minutes to defrost thoroughly before serving. The glaze can be reused by simply scraping any excess back into the container and placing it in the refrigerator.

GLAZING A CAKE

1 Place the cake you want to glaze on a wire rack set over a tray to catch the drips. Pour the glaze into the centre of the cake in one motion.

2 Keep pouring the glaze over the cake, trying to ensure the glaze runs smoothly and evenly over the entire surface and down the side of the cake.

3 Leave the glaze until it stops dripping. Trim the bottom of the cake with a small palette knife. Use the knife to lift the cake onto a serving plate.

GLAZING AN ÉCLAIR

When glazing éclairs, such as the Chocolate and tonka bean éclairs on page 101, prepare the glaze following the instructions on the opposite page, to a temperature of 35–40°C (95–104°F). Pour the glaze into a shallow container.

Take the cut tops of the éclairs and run them through the glaze, using your hand to pull them through and then lift them up vertically to allow any excess glaze to drip off.

Place the éclair tops, glaze side up, on a tray or work surface for a few minutes to set before placing the glazed tops onto the bottom halves of the éclairs.

CHERRY AND ALMOND CHEESECAKE

Serves 4–6

COMPONENTS
> Almond crumb base
> Cherry compote
> Lemon and vanilla cheesecake

This stunning and professional-looking cheesecake is simple to replicate. There are three recipes to nail before assembly, but they are all totally achievable and you can take your time as they don't have to be made together. This means you have a great looking and tasting dish without the stress. I used frozen pitted cherries, as cherries were not in season at the time, but feel free to switch up fruits as you wish – the cheesecake works well with nearly all fruits, especially berries.

ALMOND CRUMB BASE

20 g (¾ oz) plain (all-purpose) flour
20 g (¾ oz) flaked almonds
25 g (1 oz) soft light brown sugar
pinch of bicarbonate of soda
  (baking soda)
pinch of salt
25 g (1 oz) unsalted butter, melted

Preheat the oven to 170°C (340°F). Line a baking tray with baking paper.

Place the flour, almonds, sugar, bicarbonate of soda and salt in a large bowl and mix well with your fingers. Add the cooled, melted – but still liquid – butter and mix well with your fingers to form a crumble.

Press the crumble into a 15 cm (6 in) pastry ring placed on the prepared tray, and compact the crumble well with your fingers. Bake in the oven for 20–25 minutes until golden brown. Leave to cool for a couple of minutes before removing the ring.

CHERRY COMPOTE

pinch of agar agar (see page 34)
70 g (2½ oz) jam-setting sugar
  (available in most supermarkets)
500 g (1 lb 2 oz) fresh or frozen
  cherries, pitted
1 vanilla bean, seeds scraped
squeeze of lemon juice

Mix the agar agar with the sugar and stir in 100 ml (3½ fl oz) water. Add this to a saucepan with the cherries and vanilla seeds and bring to a gentle boil over medium heat. Lower to a simmer and cook for 1 minute before removing from the heat and squeezing in the lemon juice. Stir and leave to cool completely in the refrigerator before use. >

LEMON AND VANILLA CHEESECAKE

2 egg yolks
35 g (1¼ oz) caster (superfine) sugar
juice and zest of ½ lemon
2 gold-strength gelatine leaves
   (4 g/¼ oz), soaked and drained
   (see page 33)
100 g (3½ oz) cream cheese
1 vanilla bean, seeds scraped
120 ml (4 fl oz) thickened
   (whipping) cream

Place the egg yolks and sugar in the bowl of a freestanding electric mixer. Set the bowl over a saucepan of simmering water and whisk until the temperature reaches 65°C (149°F). Put the bowl back on the mixer and whisk on medium–high speed for 10 minutes.

Heat the lemon juice and gelatine in a bowl in the microwave for 30 seconds to melt then pour the mixture into the whisking eggs while the mixer is still running.

In a separate bowl, beat the cream cheese with the vanilla seeds and lemon zest.

In another bowl, whip the cream to soft peaks then fold this into the cream cheese mixture.

Fold this mixture into the egg yolks. Pour the mixture into a 15 cm (6 in) diameter pastry ring set on a lined baking tray and tap the tray gently to level the mixture in the ring.

Place in the freezer for a minimum of 4 hours to harden.

Once frozen, take the cheesecake out of the ring by warming the side of the ring with your hands.

ASSEMBLY

Take a palette knife and carefully place the frozen cheesecake on the cooked almond base. Allow the cheesecake time to defrost before topping with the cherry compote.

GREEN TEA VICTORIA SPONGE WITH LEMON BUTTER ICING

Serves 8–10

COMPONENTS
> Green tea Victoria sponge
> Lemon syrup
> Lemon frosting
> Green tea icing sugar

This is an interesting take on a classic Victoria sandwich cake. The matcha green tea works so well and I love incorporating this ingredient into my desserts as it has a beautiful flavour. To make a classic Victoria sponge you can omit the green tea powder and replace with the same weight of self-raising flour.

GREEN TEA VICTORIA SPONGE

200 g (7 oz) unsalted butter, softened
200 g (7 oz) caster (superfine) sugar
1 vanilla bean, seeds scraped
4 eggs
190 g (6½ oz) self-raising flour
1 teaspoon baking powder
25 g (1 oz) matcha green tea powder
30 ml (1 fl oz) full-cream (whole) milk

Preheat the oven to 160°C (320°F). Grease two 18 cm (7 in) diameter non-stick cake tins with canola spray. Cut circles of baking paper to fit the base of each cake tin. Place the discs of paper in the tins and spray these with canola oil.

Place the butter, sugar and vanilla seeds in a freestanding electric mixer fitted with the paddle attachment, and beat on medium speed for 10 minutes. After a couple of minutes stop the machine and scrape down the side of the bowl using a rubber spatula or scraper. Continue to beat for the full 10 minutes before adding the eggs one at a time, ensuring they are completely incorporated before adding the next one.

Sift the flour, baking powder and matcha green tea powder together into the bowl and fold them into the batter. Mix well, add the milk, mix again and transfer the batter equally between the two prepared greased tins. Smooth the surfaces of the cakes using a spatula or spoon to make them even.

Place the sponges in the oven and cook for 30–35 minutes. After 25 minutes you can open your oven to turn the sponges if needed.

The sponges are cooked when they spring back when pressed gently, or you can insert a skewer to check if the batter is still wet. If the skewer comes out clean the sponges are done.

Remove the sponges from the oven and allow them to cool in the tin for 5 minutes before running a knife around the edges to loosen the sides of the sponges from the tins. Leave to cool for a further 5 minutes before turning the sponges out onto a wire rack to cool completely. >

<

LEMON SYRUP

75 g (2¾ oz) caster (superfine) sugar
finely grated zest and juice
   of ½ lemon

Bring the sugar and 75 ml (2½ fl oz) water to a gentle boil in a saucepan over medium heat, stirring until the sugar has dissolved. Remove the pan from the heat. Stir in the lemon zest and juice. Allow the syrup to cool down completely before re-boiling and immediately straining the hot syrup into a jug through a fine sieve.

LEMON FROSTING

150 g (5½ oz) unsalted butter,
   softened
125 g (4½ oz/1 cup) icing
   (confectioners') sugar
finely grated zest of 1 lemon
30 ml (1 fl oz) full-cream (whole)
   milk

Beat the butter, sugar and lemon zest in a freestanding electric mixer fitted with the paddle attachment for 5 minutes on medium–high speed until the mixture is smooth and fluffy. Turn the mixer to low then add the milk and mix to combine.

GREEN TEA ICING SUGAR

50 g (1¾ oz) icing (confectioners')
   sugar
5 g (¼ oz) matcha green tea powder

Sift the two ingredients together into a bowl. Set aside.

ASSEMBLY

100 g (3½ oz) raspberry jam (see
   the recipe on page 52 if you would
   like to make your own)
fresh raspberries to garnish

Trim and discard a thin layer from the top of one of the sponges to even and level it out – this surface will form the inside surface of the sandwich.

Trim and discard the bottom of the other sponge to remove the brown base – this surface will be for the other inside surface of the sandwich.

Liberally brush the lemon syrup onto both sponges, primarily where they have been trimmed on the exposed sponge surfaces.

Spread the lemon frosting on the first sponge and spread the raspberry jam on the second sponge.

Sandwich the two sponges together and place the cake on a cake stand or serving plate. Dust the top of the cake with the green tea icing sugar. And garnish with fresh raspberries.

CHAPTER TWO

Tarts
& Pastries

I love a good tart and lemon is my favourite. Oh, hold on ... actually it's the white chocolate, mascarpone and pistachio one. Wait! It could be the boozy gin and tonic tarts that I have been serving my guests for years – everyone loves those when I make them. Hmm... You get the picture here. They are all quality recipes and this chapter has more than enough to get you going. I urge you to give them all a try and find your particular favourite. My guess is it will be hard to decide – oh, and did I mention my famous salted caramel is found in the wickedly addictive chocolate, caramel and hazelnut tartlets?

BAKED CUSTARD TART

Serves 12

COMPONENTS
> Sweet tart case
> Baked custard mix

Although I'm Aussie now, I was born and raised in the UK and what could be more British than custard? I just love custard in all its forms – thick with a crumble, as a hot or cold sauce or, indeed, baked like this one. The trick with this recipe is to pull the tart out of the oven at the point where it's just cooked. This takes a bit of skill and a lot of practice and will vary depending on your oven and ingredients.

SWEET TART CASE

280 g (10 oz) plain (all-purpose)
   flour
90 g (3 oz/¾ cup) icing
   (confectioners') sugar
pinch of salt
finely grated zest of ½ orange
135 g (5 oz) cold unsalted butter,
   diced
1 egg
1 egg yolk

Place the flour, icing sugar, salt and orange zest in a mixing bowl and, using your fingertips, crumble in the butter until you have a fine sandy texture.

Add the egg and egg yolk and mix again until the dough starts to come together.

Turn the dough out onto a lightly floured work surface and knead it briefly with your hands to bring it together.

Form a square shape with the dough and flatten it onto a large piece of plastic wrap. Cover the dough completely with the plastic wrap and rest it in the refrigerator for 45 minutes.

Remove the dough from the refrigerator and roll it out on a lightly floured work surface to a thickness of 2 mm (⅛ in). Roll the dough onto a sheet of baking paper on a baking tray and rest it again in the refrigerator for 20 minutes.

Preheat the oven to 170°C (340°F).

Remove the pastry from the refrigerator and use it to line a round 28 cm (11 in) non-stick tart (flan) tin. (See pages 82–3 for instructions on lining a tart tin with pastry.) You will have excess pastry, which can be frozen and reused.

Leave the tart to rest in the refrigerator for 20 minutes before blind baking the tart for 20 minutes or until cooked. (See page 83 for instructions on blind baking.) Remove the baking beans and return the tart to the oven for 2 minutes to dry out.

Leave to cool, then carefully trim excess pastry from the tart tin using a sharp knife. >

BAKED CUSTARD MIX

10 egg yolks
100 g (3½ oz) caster (superfine)
  sugar
600 ml (20½ fl oz) thickened
  (whipping) cream

Preheat the oven to 160°C (320°F).

Using an electric mixer, beat the egg yolks with the sugar until pale.

Put the cream in a saucepan over medium heat and bring to the boil.

Pour the hot cream into the egg mixture and stir to mix well. Strain the mixture through a sieve into a jug.

ASSEMBLY

whole nutmeg

Place the tart onto a shelf in the oven and pour the custard mixture into the prepared tart shell. Grate over some nutmeg using a microplane and bake the tart for 20 minutes or until cooked. Remove the tart from the oven and allow it to cool in the tin before serving.

> TIP: To make life easier, follow the method above closely, filling the tart with custard as described. It's so much easier to fill your blind-baked tart while it is already positioned in the oven rather than trying to lift a full tart. Resulting spillage will of course affect your tart and cause it to stick to the tart tin.

WHITE CHOCOLATE AND MASCARPONE TART WITH PISTACHIO NUTS

Serves 8–10

COMPONENTS
> Orange sweet tart case
> White chocolate, vanilla and mascarpone cream

As a pastry chef I am very lucky to be looked after in restaurants when I dine out, especially at dessert time. I receive gifts of extra dessert from the house – I guess because they want to see if I polish it off and because there is an unwritten rule of generosity to fellow industry professionals when they dine at each other's restaurants.

My favourite restaurant in Australia is Café Di Stasio in St Kilda and I have been going there since my arrival over 10 years ago now. My wife, Cath, introduced me to the place as she was a fan, and they have been looking after us very well ever since. They always send out a slice of white chocolate mascarpone tart at the end of our meal and it has become my favourite dessert of all time. This is my attempt at recreating the wonderful flavours and textures.

ORANGE SWEET TART CASE

280 g (10 oz) plain (all-purpose) flour
90 g (3 oz/¾ cup) icing (confectioners') sugar
pinch of salt
finely grated zest of ½ orange
135 g (5 oz) cold unsalted butter, diced
1 egg
1 egg yolk
melted white chocolate for brushing

Place the flour, icing sugar, salt, lemon zest and butter in a freestanding electric mixer fitted with the paddle attachment. Mix on low until you have a fine sandy texture.

Add the egg and egg yolk to the bowl and mix again until the dough starts to come together.

Turn the dough out onto a lightly floured work surface and knead it briefly with your hands to bring it together.

Form a square shape with the dough and flatten it on a large piece of plastic wrap. Cover the dough completely with the plastic wrap and place it in the refrigerator to chill and rest for 45 minutes.

Remove the dough from the refrigerator and roll it out on a lightly floured work surface to a thickness of 2 mm (⅛ in).

Transfer the dough to a sheet of baking paper, place it on a baking tray and rest it in the refrigerator for 20 minutes.

Remove the pastry from the refrigerator and use it to line a round 28 cm (11 in) non-stick tart (flan) tin with the pastry. (See pages 82–3 for instructions on lining tart tins with pastry.) You will have excess pastry, which can be frozen and reused.

Preheat the oven to 170°C (340°F). >

Place the tart in the refrigerator to rest for 20 minutes. Remove the tart from the refrigerator and blind bake it for 20 minutes or until cooked to a golden firm pastry. (See page 83 for instructions on blind baking.) Remove the baking beans and return the tart to the oven for 2 minutes to dry out.

Remove the tart from the oven and leave to cool in the tin. Carefully trim any excess pastry from the tin using a sharp knife. Brush the inside of the tart liberally with melted white chocolate and reserve until needed.

WHITE CHOCOLATE, VANILLA AND MASCARPONE CREAM

340 ml (11½ fl oz/1⅓ cups) thickened (whipping) cream
1 vanilla bean, seeds scraped
finely grated zest of ½ orange
1 star anise, grated
120 g (4½ oz) white chocolate, melted
100 g (3½ oz) mascarpone

Put 200 ml (7 fl oz) of the cream, the vanilla seeds, orange zest and star anise in a saucepan over medium heat. Bring to the boil then turn off the heat and leave to infuse for 10 minutes.

Bring the cream mixture back to the boil and strain it through a sieve into a bowl containing the melted white chocolate. Leave to sit for 30 seconds before stirring well with a spatula to combine.

Leave to cool for 20 minutes before folding in the mascarpone cream. Leave in a covered container in the refrigerator for a minimum of 30 minutes before use.

Remove the cream from the refrigerator and transfer it to a bowl. Add the remaining cream and whisk on medium speed to thick-ribbons, using either an electric mixer or by hand. Be careful not to over-whip this cream as it can separate quickly. Spread it into the prepared tart base.

ASSEMBLY

125 g (4½ oz) pistachio nuts, lightly toasted, coarsely chopped
100 g (3½ oz) white chocolate shards (see page 143)
finely grated zest of ½ orange
icing (confectioners') sugar for dusting

Scatter the nuts and press chocolate shards on top of the cream, standing on end, to cover it generously. Refrigerate the tart for 30 minutes.

Grate over the orange zest, dust with icing sugar and serve.

LEMON TARTS WITH RASPBERRY MARSHMALLOW

Makes 12

COMPONENTS

> Lemon sweet tart cases
> Lemon curd
> Raspberry jellies
> Raspberry marshmallow

We all love a good lemon tart and it's certainly one of my all-time favourite desserts – and I like mine on the tangy side. Of all the sweets I make, this one regularly attracts the most attention. People really seem to have a deep affection for it.

This is a fairly simple recipe as it involves pouring a curd into a tart case to set, rather than baking custard in the oven. The raspberry jellies are a gelatine and agar agar set and are easy to make and handle (see pages 34–5). Make extras and store them in the freezer for a quick raspberry burst on any dessert.

I think you will enjoy making and serving these for a long time to come and hopefully I have the tang level just as you like it.

LEMON SWEET TART CASES

280 g (10 oz) plain (all-purpose) flour
90 g (3 oz/¾ cup) icing (confectioners') sugar
pinch of salt
finely grated zest of ½ lemon
135 g (5 oz) cold unsalted butter, diced
1 egg
1 egg yolk
150g (5½ oz) melted white chocolate as needed

Place the flour, icing sugar, salt, lemon zest and butter in a freestanding electric mixer fitted with the paddle attachment. Mix on low until you have a fine sandy texture.

Add the egg and egg yolk and mix again until the dough starts to come together.

Turn the dough out onto a lightly floured work surface and knead it briefly with your hands to bring it together.

Form a square shape with the dough and flatten it on a large piece of plastic wrap. Cover the dough completely with the plastic wrap and place it in the refrigerator to chill and rest for 45 minutes.

Remove the dough from the refrigerator and roll it out on a lightly floured work surface to a thickness of 2 mm (⅛ in).

Transfer the dough onto a couple of sheets of baking paper, place them on a baking tray and rest them in the refrigerator for 20 minutes.

Preheat the oven to 170°C (340°F). Place twelve 8 x 2.5 cm (3¼ x 1 in) round tartlet moulds or rings on a baking tray (or two) lined with baking paper. >

Remove the pastry from the refrigerator and, using an 8 cm (3¼ in) round pastry cutter, cut 12 discs from the two sheets of pastry. Line the tartlet moulds with the pastry discs. (See pages 82–3 for instructions on lining tins with pastry.) Place the tarts in the refrigerator to rest for 20 minutes.

Remove the tarts from the refrigerator and trim any excess pastry from the rims. Blind bake the tarts for 20 minutes or until cooked. (See page 83 for instructions on blind baking.) Remove the baking beans and return the tarts to the oven for 2 minutes to dry out.

Remove the tarts from the oven and leave them to cool in the moulds. Turn out the tart shells and brush the insides liberally with the melted white chocolate. Reserve until needed.

LEMON CURD

8 eggs
juice and finely grated zest of
  6 lemons
260 g (9 oz) unsalted butter,
  softened
400 g (14 oz/1¾ cups) caster
  (superfine) sugar
4 gold-strength gelatine leaves
  (8 g/¼ oz), soaked and drained
  (see page 33)

Place all the ingredients, except the gelatine, in a bowl and whisk well to combine.

Place the bowl over a saucepan of simmering water and whisk the mixture constantly. Continue to cook – being careful of the steam, which can burn – and check your water does not run dry in the pan (top up the water if needed). Heat the curd until it reaches a temperature of 82°C (180°F).

Prepare a large bowl of iced water.

Remove the bowl from the saucepan on the heat and add the gelatine, stirring well until it has dissolved. Strain the curd into another bowl, then set this bowl in the larger bowl of iced water to cool the curd down quickly.

Stir the mixture occasionally over the ice to cool the curd to a temperature of 40°C (104°F). Pour the curd into the prepared tart cases and tap the tarts to level them flat.

Place the tarts in the refrigerator to finish cooling and set. This will take around 30 minutes.

> TIP: The curd can also be cooked in the microwave by placing all the ingredients, except the gelatine, in a microwave-safe bowl. Mix well and cook for 20 seconds on High (100%) then stir vigorously. Repeat these steps until the curd is starting to bubble and is smooth and shiny. Remove from the microwave and add the soaked gelatine. Mix well again then proceed with the method as above.

RASPBERRY JELLIES

200 ml (7 fl oz) raspberry purée
50 ml (1¾ fl oz) Sugar syrup (see page 13)
¼ teaspoon agar agar (see page 34)
3 gold-strength gelatine leaves (6 g/¼ oz), soaked and drained (see page 33)

Put the raspberry purée, sugar syrup and agar agar in a small saucepan over medium heat and stir to combine. Bring the mixture to the boil then remove the pan from the heat. Stir in the gelatine until it has dissolved then pour the mixture into a jug.

Pour the jelly into silicone moulds if you have them – small hemispheres work well as do greased ice cube trays. If you don't have anything suitable, pour the jelly into a lightly greased plastic container. Place in the refrigerator and allow the jelly to set for 1 hour.

Unmould the jellies. If you have set the jelly in a large container, unmould it then cut it into 1 cm (½ in) cubes.

RASPBERRY MARSHMALLOW

4 egg whites
400 g (14 oz/ 1¾ cups) caster (superfine) sugar
1 tablespoon liquid glucose
10 gold-strength gelatine leaves (20 g/¾ oz), soaked and drained (see page 33)
3 teaspoons freeze-dried raspberry powder (see page 13)

Place the egg whites in a freestanding electric mixer and start to whisk them slowly on low speed.

Place 150 ml (5 fl oz) water, the caster sugar and glucose in a small saucepan over medium heat. Stir gently to dissolve the sugar and bring the syrup to the boil.

Once the syrup has come to the boil, turn the electric mixer with the egg whites to medium speed.

Cook the syrup until it reaches a temperature of 125°C (257°F), using a digital or sugar thermometer for accuracy. Then slowly trickle the syrup in a constant stream down the side of the bowl into the whisking egg whites, ensuring it doesn't touch the whisk.

Melt the gelatine in the still-hot saucepan and add it to the bowl. Whisk well until the mixture starts to cool and thicken, then add the freeze-dried raspberry powder.

Transfer the mixture to a piping (icing) bag fitted with a small plain nozzle.

> TIP: Any left-over marshmallow can be piped into bulbs on a lightly greased baking tray for use as a garnish or extra component for any number of other desserts. They will last up to 1 week.

ASSEMBLY

12 fresh raspberries, halved

Remove the tarts filled with the curd from the refrigerator and place a couple of raspberry jellies on each tart.

Pipe about three small bulbs of marshmallow onto each tart, garnish with the halved fresh raspberries and serve.

Sweet Essentials

GREASING AND LINING TINS AND WORKING WITH PASTRY

Here are just a few tips to ensure your gorgeous baked goods can be successfully released from their tins or trays. Following these steps will also result in evenly cooked pastry that won't leak. Remember, every little detail in your cooking can make all the difference so be sure to use the correct tin, tray or ring and ensure they are greased adequately and lined neatly with baking paper, if using. If you take time and care in the rolling, lining and blind baking of your pastry you will have a greater chance of a successful final product.

LINING A ROUND CAKE TIN

Lightly spray a clean and dry tin with canola oil, ensuring all the edges and corners are lubricated. Then place the tin on a sheet of baking paper and draw around it with a pencil to mark the diameter of the tin. Cut out the paper disc to fit the inside of the tin. Place the paper disc into the base of the tin and smooth it flat with a scraper to get rid of any wrinkles. Then cut a strip of paper the length of the circumference and the height of the tin (with a couple of centimetres/an inch overhang). Gently place the strip around the inside of the tin and smooth out any wrinkles.

LINING A STRAIGHT-SIDED TIN WITH BAKING PAPER

Lightly spray a clean and dry rectangular or square baking tin with canola oil, ensuring the entire surface and all the corners are lubricated. Cut a sheet of baking paper to the exact size of the base of the tin and lay it flat in the tin. Smooth out any wrinkles in the paper using a scraper or spatula. Finally, use a sharp knife to cut any excess paper from the edges so the paper fits the tin perfectly.

ROLLING PASTRY

Once you have made your pastry and it has rested in the refrigerator, place it on a lightly floured work surface.

Work the dough with your hands to soften it to an even, manageable temperature and softness. Again lightly flour the work surface and use a rolling pin to tap the pastry to flatten it slightly as a starting point to roll the pastry.

Work quickly to roll the pastry, using flour to ensure it does not stick to the work surface or get too warm to work with.

Roll the pastry out evenly. Regularly lift the pastry from the work surface and turn it clockwise before rolling again, to ensure it stays in a round or rectangular shape. Roll the pastry out to the desired thickness.

1 Flour a work surface and quickly roll out the pastry.

2 Turn the pastry clockwise and roll it out again.

LINING A TART TIN
WITH PASTRY

To line a 35 x 12 cm (14 x 4¾ in) tart (flan) tin, you will need around 400 g (14 oz) sweet tart case dough, a rolling pin, canola spray and extra flour for dusting. A flat work surface in a cool kitchen will give you the best results.

Spray the tart tin lightly with canola oil and roll the pastry to the desired thickness. Roll the pastry over the rolling pin then unroll it over the tart tin. Gently press the pastry into the edges, patching up any holes as you go. Remove any excess pastry but don't trim the tart neat – leave some pastry overhanging. Make sure the tin is lined evenly with the pastry in all corners and edges then chill the tart tin in the freezer for 20 minutes to firm it up. Remove from the freezer and prepare your tart for blind baking (see opposite page for instructions).

LINING INDIVIDUAL TARTLET
TINS WITH PASTRY

To line individual tartlet tins you will need around 400 g (14 oz) sweet tart case dough, a rolling pin, canola spray, a flat baking tray and extra flour for dusting. A flat surface in a cool kitchen will give you the best results.

Spray the tartlet tins lightly with canola oil and roll the pastry to the desired thickness. Roll the pastry onto the rolling pin and roll it back onto the baking tray then place this in the refrigerator for 20 minutes to chill and rest. Place the tartlet tins on a baking tray.

Use a pastry cutter or similar and cut discs larger than the tartlet tins then push the pastry discs into the lightly sprayed tins, ensuring they are pushed well into the corners and evenly lined. Don't trim the excess; instead place the tartlets in the freezer for 20 minutes to firm up.

LINING INDIVIDUAL TARTLET TINS WITH PASTRY

1 Lift the cut pastry disc over the tartlet tin.

2 Gently press the pastry into the tin.

3 Ensure you have filled all the corners, but don't trim the edges yet.

BLIND BAKING

Blind baking our tarts ensures we have evenly cooked and hole-free tart shells ready to safely contain custard, curd or any other cream mix. Chilling and resting your pastry in between rolling always helps as does having your oven preheated. Remove the tart shell from the freezer and line the shells with heavy-duty plastic wrap or aluminium foil into the edges and then pour in uncooked baking beans, rice or pastry weights. Your tarts are now ready to bake in the preheated oven. You can buy baking beans and pastry weights from cooking supply stores.

Once the tarts are ready to bake, place them in the preheated oven and bake until they are just cooked. Remove the tarts from the oven and remove the baking beans or rice by lifting the plastic wrap or foil and pulling the baking beans out. Use any left-over uncooked excess pastry to plug any holes or cracks that may have appeared in the pastry and brush the inside of the tarts with egg wash. Return the tarts to the oven for 3 minutes to set the egg wash and ensure that all the holes are plugged. The tart is now ready for filling.

BLIND BAKING

1 Line the tart shells with heavy-duty plastic wrap or aluminium foil.

2 Fill the tarts with baking beans, rice or pastry weights.

3 Your tarts are now ready for the blind baking stage.

GIN AND TONIC TARTS

Makes 12

COMPONENTS
> Juniper sweet tart cases
> Fizzy white chocolate with lime
> Lime curd
> Gin and tonic jelly
> Lime marshmallow

These are so much fun! What could be better than a favourite cocktail in tart form? Make these and watch them disappear. The fizzy chocolate is a fantastic addition and the juniper in the pastry gives a familiar 'gin' aroma to the cocktail.

These can be found in my cake cabinet at Burch & Purchese Sweet Studio every day but they're especially popular with the on-the-way-home-from-work crowd on Friday evenings. I think these effervescent tarts just shout, 'The weekend is here!'

JUNIPER SWEET TART CASES

280 g (10 oz) plain (all-purpose) flour
90 g (3 oz/¾ cup) icing (confectioners') sugar
pinch of salt
½ teaspoon ground juniper
135 g (5 oz) cold unsalted butter, diced
1 egg
1 egg yolk

Place the flour, icing sugar, salt, juniper and butter in a freestanding electric mixer fitted with the paddle attachment. Mix on low speed until you have a fine sandy texture.

Add the egg and egg yolk to the bowl and mix again until the dough starts to come together.

Turn the dough out onto a lightly floured work surface and knead it briefly with your hands to bring it together.

Form a square shape with the dough and flatten it on a large piece of plastic wrap. Cover the dough completely with the plastic wrap and place it in the refrigerator to chill and rest for 45 minutes.

Remove the dough from the refrigerator and roll it out on a lightly floured work surface to a thickness of 2 mm (⅛ in).

Transfer the dough onto a couple of sheets of baking paper, place them on a tray and rest them in the refrigerator for 20 minutes.

Preheat the oven to 170°C (340°F). Place twelve 8 x 2.5 cm (3¼ x 1 in) round tartlet tins or rings on a baking tray (or two) lined with baking paper.

Remove the pastry from the refrigerator and, using an 8 cm (3¼ in) round pastry cutter, cut 12 discs from the two sheets of pastry. Line the tartlet tins with the pastry discs. (See pages 82–3 for instructions on lining tins with pastry.) Place the tarts in the refrigerator to rest for 20 minutes.

Remove the tarts from the refrigerator and trim any excess pastry from the rims. Blind bake the tarts for 20 minutes or until cooked. (See page 83 for instructions on blind baking.) Remove the baking beans and return the tarts to the oven for 2 minutes to dry out.

Remove the tarts from the oven and leave them to cool in the tin. Turn out the tarts onto a wire rack.

FIZZY WHITE CHOCOLATE WITH LIME

40 g (1½ oz/⅓ cup) icing (confectioners') sugar
40 g (1½ oz) citric acid powder
40 g (1½ oz) bicarbonate of soda (baking soda)
finely grated zest of 2 limes
340 g (12 oz) white chocolate, melted and cooled (but still liquid)

Place the icing sugar, citric acid, bicarbonate of soda and lime zest in a bowl. Add the melted chocolate and stir to combine. Set aside until cool, but keep it liquid.

Using a pastry brush, brush the chocolate mixture on the inside of the juniper sweet tart cases (see above).

The remainder of the chocolate can be spread out thinly on a clean and smooth work surface using a palette knife. Leave the chocolate to set for a few minutes before scraping it up with a metal scraper or the blade of a knife. Store the 'shavings' in a container until needed. (See page 143 for instructions on how to make chocolate shavings.)

LIME CURD

8 eggs
juice and finely grated zest of 6 limes
260 g (9 oz) unsalted butter, softened
400 g (14 oz/1¾ cups) caster (superfine) sugar
4 gold-strength gelatine leaves (8 g/¼ oz), soaked and drained (see page 33)

Place all the ingredients, except the gelatine, in a bowl and whisk well to combine. Place the bowl over a saucepan of simmering water and whisk the mixture constantly. Continue to cook – being careful of the steam, which can burn – and check your water does not run dry in the pan (top up the water if needed). Heat the curd until it reaches a temperature of 82°C (180°F), using a digital thermometer for accuracy.

Prepare a large bowl of iced water.

Remove the bowl from the saucepan on the heat and add the gelatine, stirring well until it has dissolved. Strain the curd into another bowl, then set this bowl in the larger bowl of iced water to cool the curd down quickly.

Stir the mixture occasionally over the ice to cool the curd down to a temperature of 40°C (104°F). Pour the curd into the prepared tart cases and tap the tarts gently to level them flat.

Place the tarts in the refrigerator to finish cooling and set. This will take around 30 minutes.

> TIP: The curd can also be cooked in the microwave by placing all the ingredients, except the gelatine, in a microwave-safe bowl. Mix well and cook for 20 seconds on High (100%) then stir vigorously. Repeat these steps until the curd is starting to bubble and is smooth and shiny. Remove from the microwave and add the soaked gelatine. Mix well again then proceed with the method as above. >

GIN AND TONIC JELLY

120 ml (4 fl oz) gin
350 ml (12 fl oz) tonic water
180 ml (6 fl oz) Sugar syrup (see
    page 13)
5 gold-strength gelatine leaves
    (10 g/¼ oz), soaked and drained
    (see page 33)

Mix the gin, tonic water and sugar syrup together in a bowl. Transfer to a saucepan over medium heat and gently bring to the boil.

Remove the pan from the heat and stir in the gelatine until it has dissolved.

Strain the jelly mixture through a small sieve into a plastic container and refrigerate for at least 3 hours.

LIME MARSHMALLOW

4 egg whites
400 g (14 oz/1¾ cups) caster
    (superfine) sugar
1 tablespoon liquid glucose
10 gold-strength gelatine leaves
    (20 g/¾ oz), soaked and drained
    (see page 33)
finely grated zest of 1 lime

Place the egg whites in a freestanding electric mixer and start to whisk them slowly on low speed.

Place 150 ml (5 fl oz) water, the caster sugar and glucose in a small saucepan over medium heat. Stir gently to dissolve the sugar and bring the syrup to the boil.

Once the syrup has come to the boil, turn the mixer with the egg whites to medium speed.

Cook the syrup until it reaches a temperature of 125°C (257°F), using a digital or sugar thermometer to check the temperature. Then slowly trickle the syrup in a constant stream down the side of the bowl into the whisking egg whites, ensuring it doesn't touch the whisk.

Melt the gelatine in the still-hot saucepan and add it to the bowl. Whisk well until the mixture starts to cool and thicken, then add the lime zest.

Transfer the mixture to a piping (icing) bag fitted with a small plain nozzle.

> TIP: Left-over marshmallow can be piped into bulbs on a lightly greased baking tray for use as a garnish or extra component for any number of other desserts. They will last up to 1 week.

ASSEMBLY

finely grated lime zest for garnish

Remove the tarts filled with the curd from the refrigerator. Pipe small bulbs of marshmallow onto each tart.

Place a spoon in some hot water and then scoop some gin and tonic jelly onto each tart. (See page 35 for instructions on how to spoon jelly.) Garnish the tarts with some fizzy white chocolate shavings and fresh lime zest to get the party started.

VARIATION

Try a piña colada tart – switch lime curd for pineapple; gin and tonic jelly for a Malibu jelly and remove the juniper from the pastry. Keep the lime marshmallow as is but maybe top the tarts with shaved coconut.

PEAR, GINGER AND BAKED CHOCOLATE CRUMBLE SLICE

Serves 8

COMPONENTS
> Chocolate tart case
> Roasted pears
> Chocolate and ginger cream
> Chocolate crumble

This is yummy! Crunchy and soft-centred with the warmth of the ginger and sweetness of the pear, it really hits the spot.

There are a couple of versatile components in this creation, which can be used for many other dishes or applications – for example, the crumble, which we use for the Roast pumpkin ice cream with coffee and hot chocolate sauce (page 249), and the chocolate and ginger cream can be used cooled as a cream on one of your own dessert creations.

CHOCOLATE TART CASE

250 g (9 oz/1⅔ cups) plain (all-purpose) flour
30 g (1 oz/¼ cup) Dutch (unsweetened) cocoa powder
90 g (3 oz/¾ cup) icing (confectioners') sugar
pinch of salt
135 g (5 oz) cold unsalted butter, diced
1 egg
1 egg yolk

Place the flour, cocoa powder, icing sugar and salt in a mixing bowl and, using your fingertips, crumble in the butter until you have a fine sandy texture. Add the egg and egg yolk and mix again until the dough starts to come together.

Turn the dough out onto a lightly floured work surface and knead it briefly with your hands to bring it together.

Chill and rest the dough in the refrigerator for 30 minutes. Remove the dough from the refrigerator and roll it out to a thickness of 2 mm (⅛ in). Use the pastry to line a 35 x 12 cm (14 x 4¾ in) non-stick tart tin. (See pages 82–3 for instructions on lining tins with pastry.)

Preheat the oven to 170°C (340°F).

Leave the pastry to rest in the refrigerator for 20 minutes before blind baking it for 20 minutes (it will be three-quarters cooked). (See page 83 for instructions on blind baking.)

ROASTED PEARS

2 pears
25 g (1 oz) unsalted butter, melted
40 g (1½ oz) caster (superfine) sugar

Preheat the oven to 180°C (350°F) and line a baking tray with baking paper. Peel, core and cut each pear into quarters.

Place the pear, butter and sugar in a bowl and mix well. Transfer the mixture to the prepared baking tray and roast in the oven for 30 minutes or until cooked through and beginning to go brown. Remove the pears from the oven and allow them to cool on the tray.

> TIP: You can use the poached pears from the Chocolate, pear and hazelnut cake (page 47) or even just tinned pears. >

CHOCOLATE AND GINGER CREAM

120 ml (4 fl oz) thickened
  (whipping) cream
50 ml (1¾ fl oz) full-cream (whole)
  milk, warm
10 g (¼ oz) grated fresh ginger
100 g (3½ oz) dark chocolate,
  roughly chopped
2 egg yolks
20 g (¾ oz) caster (superfine) sugar

Put the cream and milk in a saucepan over medium heat and bring
to the boil. Turn off the heat, add the grated ginger and leave to infuse
for 20 minutes.

Melt the chocolate in the microwave (see page 141).

Strain the infused milk and cream over the chocolate before stirring
to emulsify.

Whisk the egg yolks with the sugar for a minute or so by hand to
ensure the sugar has dissolved and then stir in the chocolate mixture.
Set aside.

CHOCOLATE CRUMBLE

35 g (1¼ oz) unsalted butter
45 g (1½ oz) soft light brown sugar
35 g (1¼ oz /¼ cup) plain
  (all-purpose) flour
10 g (¼ oz) Dutch (unsweetened)
  cocoa powder
pinch of bicarbonate of soda
  (baking soda)
35 g (1¼ oz/⅓ cup) ground almonds
pinch of salt

Use an electric mixer to cream the butter and sugar in a mixing bowl
until smooth.

Sift in the flour, cocoa powder and bicarbonate of soda and add the
ground almonds and salt. Mix well to form a dough. Wrap the dough
in plastic wrap and freeze for a couple of hours.

ASSEMBLY

100 g (3½ oz) block of dark
  chocolate

Preheat the oven to 150°C (300°F).

Place the roasted pear pieces in the tart case and pour over the
chocolate and ginger cream filling to come to the top of the tart. Bake
for 20 minutes before removing the tart from the oven and turning
the oven up to 170°C (340°F).

Grate around half of the frozen chocolate crumble evenly over the
surface of the tart and return the tart to the oven to bake for a further
25 minutes.

Remove the tart from the oven and leave it to cool in the tin. Remove
from the tin once cool, and generously grate some dark chocolate on
top. Slice and serve.

BAKEWELL TART

Serves 8

COMPONENTS
> Almond cream
> Sweet tart case

During the shoot for this book I was trying to decide how to finish this tart when my wife, Cath, arrived home with the most amazing fruit from the market. There were juicy figs, amazing strawberries, nectarines and plums and I thought let's just use these and not try too hard. The result was better than anything I could have spent days working on – the produce speaks for itself and the tart is extremely simple to put together. You're not limited to using these fruits. Just pop down to your local market and see what looks great and it's sure to work well.

ALMOND CREAM

60 g (2 oz) unsalted butter,
  at room temperature
pinch of salt
1 vanilla bean, seeds scraped
finely grated zest of ½ lemon
60 g (2 oz/½ cup) icing
  (confectioners') sugar, sifted
60 g (2 oz) ground almonds
1 egg
10 g (¼ oz) plain (all-purpose) flour

Place the butter, salt, vanilla seeds, lemon zest, icing sugar and ground almonds in a freestanding electric mixer fitted with the paddle attachment and mix on low speed until the paste is smooth and well incorporated.

Use a spatula or scraper to scrape the paste from the inside of the bowl and mix well again.

Add the egg and mix it in well before adding the flour. >

SWEET TART CASE

280 g (10 oz) plain (all-purpose)
  flour
90 g (3 oz/¾ cup) icing
  (confectioners') sugar
pinch of salt
1 vanilla bean, seeds scraped
135 g (5 oz) cold unsalted butter,
  diced
1 egg
1 egg yolk
50 g (1¾ oz) apricot jam (see the
  recipe on page 52 if you'd like to
  make your own)

Place the flour, icing sugar, salt and vanilla seeds in a mixing bowl and, using your fingertips, crumble in the butter until you have a fine sandy texture.

Add the egg and egg yolk and mix again until the dough starts to come together. Turn it out onto a lightly floured work surface and knead it briefly with your hands to bring it together.

Chill and rest the dough in the refrigerator for 45 minutes before rolling it out on a lightly floured work surface to a thickness of 2 mm (⅛ in). Roll the dough onto a sheet of baking paper on a baking tray and rest in the refrigerator for 20 minutes.

Remove the pastry from the refrigerator and use it to line a 35 x 12 cm (14 x 4¾ in) non-stick tart mould. (See pages 82–3 for instructions on lining a tin with pastry.) You will have excess pastry, which can be frozen and reused.

Preheat the oven to 170°C (340°F).

Place the tart in the refrigerator to rest for 20 minutes before trimming any excess pastry from the rim. Blind bake the tart for 15 minutes or until nearly cooked. (See page 83 for instructions on blind baking.) Remove the baking beans and leave the tart to cool before spreading the jam evenly onto the base.

ASSEMBLY

fresh seasonal fruit (I used
  nectarines, plums, strawberries
  and figs), cut into chunks

Spread the almond cream onto the tart, over the top of the jam, up to about a couple of millimetres (⅛ in) from the top.

Push the chunks of fruit into the almond cream.

Place the tart back in the oven and bake for 25–30 minutes until golden brown. Remove from the oven and leave to cool completely before unmoulding and serving.

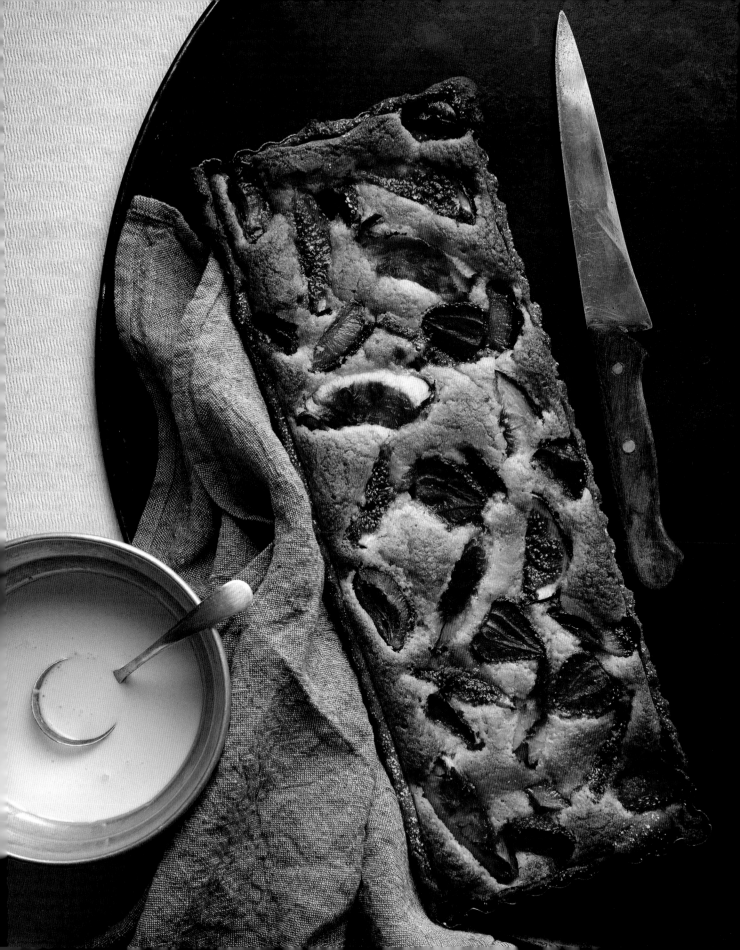

Sweet Essentials

SALTED CARAMEL

This simply has to be one of the greatest food pairings of all time – the sweetness of caramel is cut and skilfully tempered with the use of salt. At my Sweet Studio in Melbourne we make 80 litres (21 gallons) of the stuff a week and the job has got so big that we now have a machine to take care of all the hard work. This recipe is as close as possible to the one I make in the shop and I have developed it to work in your kitchen at home. Once you have mastered this you can easily whip up a few of my amazing Chocolate and salted caramel tarts with caramelised hazelnuts (page 97), plus you can drizzle, spread and scoop your way to baking success.

Tips for a smooth, sweet and salty caramel

> Ensure your tools are spotlessly clean, including your whisk, the saucepan, the sieve and the tip of your thermometer.

> Use the thermometer to accurately check the cooking temperature to ensure the viscosity of your caramel will be just right once cool.

> Use a saucepan of sufficient size to ensure the mixture does not boil over during cooking.

SALTED CARAMEL

450 ml (15 fl oz) thickened (whipping) cream
200 g (7 oz) caster (superfine) sugar
1 vanilla bean, seeds scraped
8 g (¼ oz) salt
100 ml (3½ fl oz) liquid glucose
45 g (1½ oz) unsalted butter

1 Place 250 ml (8½ fl oz/1 cup) of the cream, along with the sugar, vanilla seeds, salt and glucose in a saucepan over medium heat.

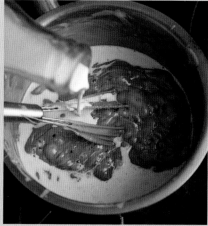

2 Remove the caramel from the heat and whisk in the remaining cream.

3 Ensure you whisk the cream in well.

4 Add the butter and whisk to combine.

5 Continue to whisk until you have a smooth and golden caramel.

6 Strain the caramel and leave to cool at room temperature. Allow it to cool thoroughly before use.

CHOCOLATE AND SALTED CARAMEL TARTS WITH CARAMELISED HAZELNUTS

Makes 24

COMPONENTS

> Chocolate tart cases
> Salted caramel (page 94)
> Chocolate tart filling
> Chocolate-coated caramelised
  hazelnuts (page 163)

This recipe makes 24 because, seriously, one is just not enough of these luscious tarts! They are great to make for a party or a get together and the salted caramel is addictive, salty sweet liquid gold. You can make smaller tarts if you have smaller tins but I would not recommend trying to make these any bigger. Once you bite into them, the caramel will not stop flowing so bigger tarts mean you have to eat the whole thing – and you know what they say about too much of a good thing.

CHOCOLATE TART CASES

250 g (9 oz/1⅔ cups) plain
  (all-purpose) flour
30 g (1 oz/¼ cup) Dutch
  (unsweetened) cocoa powder
90 g (3 oz/¾ cup) icing
  (confectioners') sugar
pinch of salt
135 g (5 oz) cold unsalted butter,
  diced
1 egg
1 egg yolk
250 g (9 oz) dark chocolate, melted

Place the flour, cocoa powder, icing sugar, salt and butter in a freestanding electric mixer fitted with the paddle attachment. Mix on low speed until you have a fine sandy texture.

Add the egg and egg yolk to the bowl and mix again until the dough starts to come together.

Turn the dough out onto a lightly floured work surface and knead it briefly with your hands to bring it together. Chill and rest the dough in the refrigerator for 30 minutes.

Remove the dough from the refrigerator and roll it out on a lightly floured work surface to a thickness of 2 mm (⅛ in).

Line twenty-four 6 x 2.5 cm (2½ x 1 in) round tartlet tins with the pastry. Use non-stick or lightly greased tins. (See pages 82–3 for instructions on lining tins with pastry.)

Preheat the oven to 165°C (330°F).

Place the tarts on a baking tray and chill in the refrigerator for 20 minutes. Remove the tarts from the refrigerator and trim them with a sharp knife if necessary. Blind bake them for 20 minutes or until cooked to firm pastry. (See page 83 for instructions on blind baking.) Remove the baking beans and return the tarts to the oven for 5 minutes to dry out.

Remove the tarts from the oven and leave them to cool in the tin. Turn out the tarts and brush the insides liberally with the melted chocolate. Reserve until needed. >

<

CHOCOLATE TART FILLING

170 g (6 oz) dark chocolate,
  roughly chopped
65 g (2¼ oz) unsalted butter,
  at room temperature
185 ml (6 fl oz) thickened
  (whipping) cream
20 ml (¾ fl oz) liquid glucose

Put the chocolate and butter in a mixing bowl.

Place the cream and glucose in a saucepan over medium heat and bring to the boil.

Pour the hot cream over the chocolate and butter and stir to combine with a spatula. Work slowly, stirring from the middle of the bowl to the outside to ensure the chocolate has melted. You should have a smooth shiny cream.

Pour the mixture into a jug. If it becomes too thick to use, you can warm it gently in the microwave before use – you need the mixture to be fluid to set level.

> TIPS: If a slight separation appears then you can emulsify the chocolate filling with a hand-held blender until it is smooth and shiny. I recommend making the chocolate filling a couple of hours before (or at least on the day) you want to serve the tarts. Any excess filling can be left to set and then scooped into a piping (icing) bag to use for decoration or another dessert.

ASSEMBLY

Salted caramel, cooled
Chocolate-coated caramelised
  hazelnuts, some crushed
chocolate curls dusted with
  unsweetened (Dutch) cocoa
  powder (see pages 142–3)
grated dark chocolate for garnish

Transfer the cooled caramel to a piping (icing) bag fitted with a large plain nozzle. Pipe (or simply spoon) the cooled caramel halfway into each chocolate-brushed tart. Leave for 20 minutes to settle and flatten.

Pour the chocolate tart mixture on top of the caramel, filling the tarts right to the top. Tap the tarts gently to level the surface.

Allow the tarts to set at room temperature for 15 minutes before topping with crushed and whole caramelised hazelnuts, chocolate curls and some extra grated dark chocolate. Serve almost immediately.

> TIPS: You can make the tarts, salted caramel and garnishes in advance and even fill your tart shells with caramel a day ahead – or freeze them filled with caramel. If freezing, remove them from the freezer and leave to thaw before using. Make the chocolate tart filling and pour it in.

I don't recommend placing the tarts in the refrigerator as it changes the luscious texture of the chocolate filling, but you can do so if necessary. Just pull them out an hour before serving to let the filling thaw to a softer consistency.

CHOCOLATE AND TONKA BEAN ÉCLAIRS

Makes 6

COMPONENTS
> Baked chocolate éclairs
> Chocolate custard cream
> Tonka-infused white chocolate cream
> Dark chocolate glaze (see page 57)

Tonka beans are extremely fragrant and I believe toxic in large doses. Don't be put off by this, though. In small quantities they are harmless and they provide an amazing aromatic flavour that takes these éclairs to the next level. If you can't find tonka beans at specialist food stores or online, then replace them with the seeds from a vanilla bean.

BAKED CHOCOLATE ÉCLAIRS

200 ml (7 fl oz) cold water
95 g (3¼ oz) unsalted butter
large pinch of salt
large pinch of sugar
15 g (½ oz) skim milk powder
80 g (2¾ oz) plain (all-purpose) flour, sifted
30 g (1 oz/¼ cup) Dutch (unsweetened) cocoa powder, sifted
4 eggs

Put the water, butter, salt and sugar in a large heavy-based saucepan over medium heat and bring to the boil ensuring the butter has melted. While boiling, whisk in the milk powder to dissolve it.

Remove the pan from the heat and dump in the flour and cocoa powder all in one go, then stir with a rubber spatula or wooden spoon.

Place the pan back over medium heat and continue to stir with the spatula. Cook the mixture for around 2 minutes until the dough starts to form a ball and leaves the side of the pan.

Transfer the dough to a freestanding electric mixer fitted with the paddle attachment. Mix on medium–high speed for 20 seconds to release some of the steam and cool the dough slightly. Add the eggs, mixing well after each addition. The batter should be thick and glossy.

Transfer the pastry to a shallow container and cover with plastic wrap. Cool in the refrigerator for 1 hour before transferring to a piping (icing) bag fitted with a large fluted or plain nozzle.

Using a ruler as a guide, pipe the choux pastry into lengths of 26 cm (10¼ in) on a tray lined with baking paper. Place the tray in the freezer to chill for a couple of hours.

Once hard, remove the pastry from the freezer and transfer each piece of choux to a chopping board. Use a knife and a ruler to cut two 12 cm (4¾ in) lengths from each piece. Discard any trim and store the éclairs back in the freezer. You can now pull out as many as you want to cook.

Preheat the oven to 165°C (330°F) and line a baking tray with baking paper. >

< Place six éclairs on the prepared baking tray, spaced evenly apart and let the éclairs thaw.

Place the tray in the oven and bake for 20 minutes. Do not open the door while baking as this may cause a collapse in your pastry. Reduce the oven temperature to 160°C (320°F) and bake for a further 20 minutes. Turn the oven off completely and leave the éclairs in the oven to dry out for a further 20 minutes. Remove from the oven and place them on a wire rack to cool completely before filling.

CHOCOLATE CUSTARD CREAM

3 egg yolks
15 g (½ oz) caster (superfine) sugar
110 ml (4 fl oz) full-cream (whole) milk
110 ml (4 fl oz) thickened (whipping) cream
120 g (4½ oz) dark chocolate, roughly chopped

Using an electric mixer, beat the egg yolks and sugar together in a bowl until the sugar has dissolved and the mixture has paled.

Place the milk and cream in a saucepan over medium heat and bring to the boil. Pour the hot mixture over the eggs and sugar. Mix well and transfer to a clean saucepan over low heat.

Cook the custard until it reaches a temperature of 82°C (180°F). Use a digital thermometer to accurately check the temperature.

Put the chocolate in a bowl.

Once the custard has reached temperature, pour it over the chocolate. Leave to sit for 20 seconds before mixing well to form a smooth shiny cream. Store in the refrigerator for a minimum of 1 hour before use.

TONKA-INFUSED WHITE CHOCOLATE CREAM

555 ml (19 fl oz) thickened (whipping) cream
½ tonka bean (or vanilla bean if you can't find tonka)
270 g (9½ oz) white chocolate, melted

Put 180 ml (6 fl oz) of the cream in a saucepan over medium heat and bring it to the boil. Remove the pan from the heat and grate in the tonka bean using a microplane.

Put the melted white chocolate in a bowl.

Leave the cream to infuse for 1 hour before re-boiling and straining the cream through a fine sieve over the melted white chocolate. Let it sit for 30 seconds before stirring well with a spatula to combine.

Stir in the remaining cold cream. Transfer the mixture to a covered container and place in the refrigerator for a minimum of 1 hour before use.

Whisk the cream to thick ribbons using an electric mixer or hand whisk. Be careful not to over-whip this cream as it can separate quickly.

Transfer the cream to a piping (icing) bag fitted with a large plain nozzle.

ASSEMBLY

Dark chocolate glaze
Dutch (unsweetened) cocoa
 powder for dusting

Remove the top one-third of each éclair using a sharp paring or serrated knife. Reserve the tops and scoop out any soft filling from the éclair bottoms to leave a clean cavity.

Pipe or spoon the chocolate custard cream into each cavity until almost full.

Pipe bulbs of the tonka cream along the éclairs on the chocolate custard cream.

Dip the outside surface of the reserved éclair 'lids' through the dark chocolate glaze then use the lids to top the piped éclairs. Leave to set at room temperature. (See page 61 for instructions on dipping éclairs in chocolate.)

Lightly dust with cocoa powder and serve.

LEMON MERINGUE PIE ÉCLAIRS

Makes 6

COMPONENTS
> Baked éclairs
> Lemon curd
> Italian meringue

I love éclairs – they're a bit posh and you can fill them with anything.

You don't have to cut the tops off as shown here – you can fill éclairs by making holes in the base and filling them with cream in a piping (icing) bag. The choux pastry is also great for making profiteroles or you can fill them with cheesy sauce for a savoury gougère.

Get inventive with your éclairs, don't just stick to the same type. Use some of the recipes in this book to come up with your own unique creations – think lamington éclairs, carrot cake éclairs or even fill them with ice cream!

BAKED ÉCLAIRS

200 ml (7 fl oz) cold water
95 g (3¼ oz) unsalted butter
large pinch of salt
large pinch of sugar
15 g (½ oz) skim milk powder
110 g (4 oz/¾ cup) plain
  (all-purpose) flour, sifted
4 eggs

Put the water, butter, salt and sugar in a large heavy-based saucepan over medium heat and bring to the boil, ensuring the butter has melted. While boiling, whisk in the milk powder to dissolve it.

Remove the pan from the heat and add the flour to the pan all in one go then stir with a rubber spatula or wooden spoon.

Place the pan back over medium heat. Continue to stir with the spatula and cook the mixture for around 2 minutes until the dough starts to form a ball and leaves the side of the pan.

Transfer the dough to a freestanding electric mixer fitted with the paddle attachment. Mix on medium–high speed for 20 seconds to release some of the steam and cool the dough slightly. Add the eggs, one at a time, beating well after each addition. The batter should be thick and glossy.

Transfer it to a shallow container and cover with plastic wrap. Chill the pastry in the refrigerator for 1 hour before transferring it to a piping (icing) bag fitted with a large fluted or plain nozzle.

Using a ruler as a guide, pipe the choux pastry into lengths of 26 cm (10¼ in) onto a tray lined with baking paper.

Pipe all of the choux and place the tray in the freezer to chill for a couple of hours until hard. >

Remove from the freezer and transfer each piece of choux onto a chopping board. Use a knife and ruler to cut two 12 cm (4¾ in) lengths from each piece. Discard any trim and store the éclairs back in the freezer. You can now pull out as many as you want to cook.

Preheat the oven to 165°C (330°F) and line a baking tray with baking paper.

Place six éclairs on the prepared baking tray, spaced evenly apart, and leave them to thaw.

Place the tray in the oven and bake for 20 minutes. Do not open the door while baking as this may cause a collapse in your pastry. Reduce the oven temperature to 160°C (320°F) and bake for a further 20 minutes. Turn the oven off completely and leave the éclairs in the oven to dry out for a further 20 minutes. Remove them from the oven and place them on a wire rack to cool completely before filling.

LEMON CURD

4 eggs
juice and finely grated zest of
  3 lemons
130 g (4½ oz) unsalted butter,
  softened
200 g (7 oz) caster (superfine)
  sugar
4 gold-strength gelatine leaves
  (8 g/¼ oz), soaked and drained
  (see page 33)

Place all the ingredients, except the gelatine, in a bowl and whisk well to combine.

Place the bowl over a saucepan of simmering water and whisk the mixture constantly.

Continue to cook and heat – being careful of the steam, which can burn – and check your water does not run dry in the pan. Top up the water if needed. Heat the curd until it reaches a temperature of 82°C (180°F), using a digital thermometer to accurately check the temperature.

Once the temperature has been reached, remove the bowl from the water bath and add the gelatine, mixing well to dissolve it before straining the curd into a bowl.

Prepare a large bowl of iced water.

Place the bowl of curd in the larger bowl of iced water to cool the curd down quickly, stirring the mixture occasionally. Store in the refrigerator until needed.

> TIP: The curd can also be cooked in the microwave by placing all the ingredients, except the gelatine, in a microwave-safe bowl. Mix well and place in the microwave. Cook for 20 seconds on High (100%) and stir vigorously. Repeat these steps until the curd is starting to bubble and is smooth and shiny. Remove from the microwave and add the gelatine, stirring to dissolve. Proceed with the method above.

ITALIAN MERINGUE

200 g (7 oz) caster (superfine)
  sugar
4 egg whites

Place the sugar and 150 ml (5 fl oz) water in a small saucepan over medium heat.

At the same time, put the egg whites in a freestanding electric mixer and start to whisk slowly on low speed.

Bring the syrup to the boil then continue cooking until it reaches a temperature of 112°C (234°F), using a digital or sugar thermometer to check the temperature. Turn the electric mixer speed to medium–high.

Continue cooking the syrup, using a digital thermometer to accurately check the temperature. When the temperature reaches 121°C (250°F), remove the pan from the heat and slowly trickle the syrup down the side of the whisking bowl, ensuring it does not hit the whisk. Once all the syrup is in, beat the meringue on high speed for 10 minutes to cool. The meringue should be thick and glossy. (See page 239 for step-by-step instructions on how to make Italian meringue.)

ASSEMBLY

white chocolate shavings
  (see page 143)

Remove the top one-third of each éclair using a sharp paring or serrated knife. Discard the tops and scoop out any excess moist pastry from the bottom of the éclairs to leave a clean cavity.

Beat the lemon curd by hand until smooth, using a spatula. Transfer it to a piping (icing) bag fitted with a plain nozzle. Pipe curd into each of the éclairs to fill the cavities.

Transfer the Italian meringue to a piping bag fitted with a plain nozzle and decorate the éclairs.

Lightly glaze the meringue using a blowtorch to caramelise the edges of the piping. Serve garnish with white chocolate shavings.

RASPBERRY, LYCHEE AND ROSE CHOUX BUNS

Makes 10 buns

COMPONENTS
> Baked choux buns
> White chocolate and rose cream
> Crystallised rose petals

Elegant and feminine, these make a beautiful late-morning or afternoon treat with a cup of tea. I love having friends around and serving these – they always get a 'wow' reaction.

The white chocolate cream is such an amazing recipe and is used throughout this book. I love it for its flavour, richness and the fact that it has a longer shelf life than a pastry cream made with eggs. It is super easy and also versatile as it can be whipped and flavoured many ways – the rose here is just one example.

BAKED CHOUX BUNS

160 ml (5½ fl oz) cold water
75 g (2¾ oz) cold butter, diced
5 g (¼ oz) salt
15 g (½ oz) caster (superfine) sugar
20 g (¾ oz) skim milk powder
90 g (3 oz) plain (all-purpose) flour, sifted
3 eggs

Preheat the oven to 190°C (375°F). Spray a baking tray lightly with canola oil and lay a sheet of baking paper on top to stick. Smooth the paper flat.

Combine the cold water, butter, salt and sugar in a large saucepan over high heat and bring to the boil. While boiling, whisk in the milk powder to dissolve it.

Reduce the heat to medium then add the sifted flour all in one go, while stirring with a rubber spatula or wooden spoon. Continue to cook and stir for around 2 minutes until the mixture comes together to form a ball and forms a slight skin at the base of the pan.

Transfer the dough to a freestanding electric mixer fitted with the paddle attachment and mix on low–medium speed for about 30 seconds to release some of the steam and cool the dough down slightly. Add the eggs, one at a time, mixing well after each addition.

Transfer the mixture to a piping (icing) bag fitted with a large plain nozzle. Pipe 10 equal-sized bulbs, evenly spaced, on the lined baking tray. Each bulb should be around the size of a golf ball.

Wet your finger with cold water and use it to smooth the top of each bun to ensure they are all even and look the same. (At this point the buns can be rested in the refrigerator or even frozen for later use.)

Place the buns in the oven and bake for 20 minutes. Do not open the door while baking as this may cause a collapse in your pastry. Reduce the oven temperature to 160°C (320°F) and bake for a further 20 minutes. >

Turn the oven off completely and leave the buns in the oven to dry out for a further 20 minutes. Remove the buns from the oven and place them on a wire rack to cool completely before filling.

> TIP: Freeze the buns, unbaked, on the tray for 4 hours until completely hard and then store them, covered, in a plastic container. When needed, remove them from the freezer and place them on a tray lined with baking paper. Allow them to defrost at room temperature for 1 hour before following the baking instructions in the recipe.

WHITE CHOCOLATE AND ROSE CREAM

120 g (4½ oz) white chocolate, melted
1 vanilla bean, seeds scraped
240 ml (8 fl oz) thickened (whipping) cream
35 ml (1¼ fl oz) rosewater

Put the chocolate and vanilla seeds in a bowl.

Put 80 ml (2½ fl oz/⅓ cup) of the cream in a saucepan over medium heat and bring to the boil.

Pour the hot cream over the chocolate and vanilla. Leave to sit for 30 seconds before stirring well with a spatula to combine. Stir in the remaining cold cream.

Transfer the mixture to a covered container and place in the refrigerator for a minimum of 1 hour before using.

Whisk the cream to thick ribbons using an electric mixer or hand whisk, then add the rosewater. Be careful not to over-whip this cream as it can separate quickly.

Transfer the cream to a piping (icing) bag fitted with a large fluted nozzle.

CRYSTALLISED ROSE PETALS

50 ml (1¾ fl oz) rosewater
½ gold-strength gelatine leaf (1 g/¹⁄₁₆ oz), soaked and drained (see page 33)
1 egg white
30 edible unsprayed rose petals
caster (superfine) sugar for dusting

Heat the rosewater in the microwave for 20 seconds on High (100%) then stir in the gelatine until it has dissolved.

Whisk the egg white by hand in a bowl and slowly incorporate the rosewater–gelatine mixture. Continue to whisk until the mixture froths up.

Brush this mixture delicately onto a rose petal, ensuring it is fully covered but not drenched. Toss the petal in the sugar and shake to cover completely. Remove the petal and place it on a baking tray lined with baking paper.

Repeat with the remaining petals and place the completed tray on a windowsill or in a warm place for a couple of hours to crystallise. Store the dried petals in a covered dry container until needed.

ASSEMBLY

melted white chocolate, cooled
(but still liquid)
raspberry jam (see the recipe on
page 52 if you'd like to make
your own)
50–60 frozen or fresh raspberries
halved lychee pieces
icing (confectioners') sugar for
dusting
freeze-dried raspberry powder
(see page 13)

Pick up a baked bun and dip the bottom half into the cooled melted white chocolate and shake off the excess. Place the bun on a tray lined with baking paper. Repeat with the remainder of the buns.

Cut each of the choux buns in half horizontally and scoop out any excess moist pastry from both halves.

Spoon a teaspoon of raspberry jam into the base of each bottom half of the buns.

Arrange five or six frozen or fresh raspberries on top of the jam and then add pieces of lychee to the buns.

Pipe the white chocolate and rose cream evenly in a rosette shape into all of the buns on top of the fruit.

Lightly dust the top of each top half of the choux buns with icing sugar and place them on top of the cream.

Serve with two or three crystallised rose petals on each bun and a dusting of freeze-dried raspberry powder.

PEANUT BUTTER AND JAM CHOCOLATE ICE CREAM PROFITEROLES

Makes 6

All of the major food groups are well represented here – chocolate, ice cream, peanut butter, caramel and jam. Enjoy!

COMPONENTS
> Chocolate chip ice cream
> Baked chocolate choux bun
> Peanut butter caramel
  (see page 158)

CHOCOLATE CHIP ICE CREAM

500 g (1 lb 2 oz) Chocolate ice
  cream (see page 22)
30 g (1 oz) dark chocolate,
  roughly chopped

Prepare the chocolate ice cream following the instructions on page 22. Place the chocolate ice cream in a bowl and leave for 5 minutes to soften. Add the chocolate pieces and mix well with a spatula. Store in the freezer until required.

BAKED CHOCOLATE CHOUX BUNS

160 ml (5½ fl oz) cold water
75 g (2¾ oz) cold butter, diced
5 g (¼ oz) salt
15 g (½ oz) caster (superfine) sugar
20 g (¾ oz) skim milk powder
70 g (2½ oz) plain (all-purpose)
  flour, sifted
20 g (¾ oz) Dutch (unsweetened)
  cocoa powder, sifted
3 eggs

Preheat the oven to 190°C (375°F). Spray a baking tray lightly with canola oil and lay a sheet of baking paper on top to stick. Smooth the paper flat.

Combine the cold water, butter, salt and sugar in a large saucepan over high heat and bring to the boil. While boiling, whisk in the milk powder to dissolve it.

Reduce the heat to medium then add the sifted flour and cocoa powder all in one go while stirring with a rubber spatula or wooden spoon. Continue to cook and stir for around 2 minutes until the mixture comes together to form a ball and forms a slight skin at the base of the pan.

Transfer the dough to a freestanding mixer fitted with the paddle attachment and mix on low–medium speed for about 30 seconds to release some of the steam and cool the dough off slightly. Add the eggs one at a time, beating well after each addition.

Transfer the mixture to a piping (icing) bag fitted with a large plain nozzle. Pipe six equal-sized bulbs, evenly spaced apart, on the lined baking tray. Each bulb should be the size of a large golf ball. >

Wet your finger with cold water and use it to smooth the top of each bun to ensure they are all even and look the same.

Freeze the buns, unbaked, on the tray for 4 hours until completely hard and then store them, covered, in a plastic container in the freezer until needed.

Remove the buns from the freezer and place them on a baking tray lined with baking paper. Allow them to defrost at room temperature for 1 hour.

Place the tray in the oven and bake for 20 minutes. Do not open the door while baking as this may cause a collapse in your pastry. Reduce the oven temperature to 160°C (320°F) and bake for a further 20 minutes.

Turn the oven off completely and leave the buns in the oven to dry out for a further 20 minutes. Remove the buns from the oven and place them on a wire rack to cool completely before filling.

ASSEMBLY

300 g (10½ oz) dark chocolate, roughly chopped
200 g (7 oz) raspberry jam (see the recipe on page 52 if you'd like to make your own)
peanut butter to taste
crushed toasted peanuts for garnish

Use a small serrated knife to cut the buns in half horizontally.

Melt the chocolate in the microwave (see page 141).

First spoon some raspberry jam and then some peanut butter into the base of each baked chocolate choux bun.

Scoop a large ball of chocolate ice cream into each bun and spoon over some peanut butter caramel.

Top with the bun lid and pour over the melted chocolate followed by crushed toasted peanuts over the top.

CHAPTER THREE

Breakfasts, Biscuits & Sweet Treats

This chapter has all the bases covered –
from delicious treats for brekkie, including
the best-looking pancakes ever, to quite
possibly the best-ever toasted sandwich, to
some of my favourite biscuits. Some classic
and some new-school baked goods are here
and you can contrast the past with the
present by making my classic madeleines
and my explosive raspberry wagon wheels.
Confections are found here too, so you
can try your hand at Burch & Purchese's
signature popcorn and honeycomb rubble.
To finish on a super sugar high, you can
wash it all down with some decadent
chocolate milk.

HONEY-BAKED GRANOLA WITH YOGHURT AND ROASTED STRAWBERRIES

Serves 4 (with left-over granola to enjoy during the week)

COMPONENTS
> Honey-baked granola
> Roasted strawberries

The recipe for this is one of the most requested by visitors to my shop. It's healthy and not too sweet with a nice balance of ingredients to get your day off to a great start. The roasted strawberries are a revelation – mind-blowing flavour is extracted from everyday strawberries after just 20 minutes in the oven. A tip on the ingredients, if you can't find all of them, it's not the end of the world. Just use a replacement. Make a big batch of granola for a quick breakfast every day.

HONEY-BAKED GRANOLA

50 g (1¾ oz) puffed quinoa
80 g (2¾ oz) cocoa nibs
600 g (1 lb 5 oz/6 cups) rolled (porridge) oats
200 g (7 oz) sunflower seeds
100 g (3½ oz) pepitas (pumpkin seeds)
100 g (3½ oz/⅔ cup) sesame seeds
200 g (7 oz) almonds, skin on, coarsely chopped
100 g (3½ oz) walnuts, coarsely chopped
1 teaspoon salt
1 teaspoon ground cinnamon
1 teaspoon ground ginger
150 g (5½ oz) unsalted butter
400 g (14 oz) honey
100 g (3½ oz) dried cranberries
100 g (3½ oz) sultanas (golden raisins)
100 g (3½ oz/⅔ cup) currants
20 g (¾ oz) freeze-dried strawberry slices (see page 13)
100 g (3½ oz) flaked coconut

Preheat the oven to 170°C (340°F).

Mix the puffed quinoa, cocoa nibs, oats, sunflower seeds, pepitas, sesame seeds, almonds, walnuts, salt and spices together well in a large bowl.

Heat the butter in a large saucepan over medium heat to melt it and add the honey. Bring to the boil then pour this hot mixture over the dried ingredients in the bowl, mixing well with a wooden spoon or spatula – or in a freestanding electric mixer fitted with the paddle attachment.

Spread the granola 1 cm (½ in) thick and evenly onto baking trays lined with baking paper and bake for 18 minutes or until golden-brown. Make sure the granola is cooked sufficiently to ensure you get crunchy clusters.

Leave to cool on the trays then break up the granola pieces in a container with the remaining ingredients and mix well. You can keep the granola in a sealed container in your pantry for up to a couple of months. >

<

ROASTED STRAWBERRIES

800 g (1 lb 12 oz/5⅓ cups)
  strawberries

Preheat the oven to 170°C (340°F).

Wash, hull and halve the strawberries and place them straight onto a baking tray. Roast the strawberries in the oven for 20 minutes.

Remove them from the oven and leave to cool for 10 minutes.

TO SERVE

Greek-style yoghurt

Serve the granola topped with the strawberries and thick yoghurt on the side. Add additional honey if you need a little more sweetness.

BIRCHER MUESLI

Serves 4–6

225 g (8 oz/2¼ cups) rolled
  (porridge) oats
500 ml (17 fl oz/2 cups) full-cream
  (whole) milk
2 apples (skin on), grated
juice and finely grated zest of
  1 lemon
75 g (2¾ oz) honey
40 g (1½ oz/⅓ cup) sultanas (golden
  raisins)
150 g (5½ oz) plain yoghurt
75 g (2¾ oz/½ cup) strawberries,
  hulled and mashed
25 g (1 oz) hazelnuts or almonds,
  flaked
1 orange, segmented
75 g (2¾ oz) frozen raspberries

Another-time saver in the morning, as this is prepared the night before. Loads of fresh, healthy flavours and a blend of crunchy, chewy and smooth, this really gives you the energy to face a busy day. Again you can switch ingredients to put your own spin on this.

Soak the oats in the milk and leave to stand for 20 minutes.

Mix the grated apple with the lemon juice and zest.

Combine all the ingredients and refrigerate overnight before serving.

ROASTED PINEAPPLE PANCAKES

Serves 4

four 1 cm (½ in) pineapple slices,
   thick core removed
icing (confectioners') sugar for
   dusting
170 g (6 oz) plain (all-purpose) flour
10 g (¼ oz) baking powder
pinch of bicarbonate of soda
   (baking soda)
30 g (1 oz) caster (superfine) sugar
1 teaspoon salt
200 ml (7 fl oz) full-cream (whole)
   milk
3 eggs
30 g (1 oz) unsalted butter, cold
   melted
Passionfruit curd (see page 221)
   to serve
fresh passionfruit pulp to garnish

These are fun to make with the kids. Help them make the batter the night before – tell them both they and the batter need rest overnight to be at their best the next day. I've used pineapple for a cool new take on the humble pancake, but blueberries work just as well. Really though, the options for toppings and fillings are almost endless.

Dust each side of the pineapple slices well with the icing sugar.

Sift the flour, baking powder and bicarbonate of soda together in a bowl. Add the sugar and salt and mix to combine.

Slowly mix in the milk, then the eggs, one at a time, mixing well after each addition, and lastly the cooled melted butter. Pass the mixture through a sieve into a container. Rest the batter in the refrigerator for a minimum of 1 hour.

Spray a non-stick frying pan with canola oil and place it over medium–low heat. Cook a slice of pineapple for a couple of minutes on each side to caramelise. Remove the pineapple from the pan and clean the pan with paper towel. Spray again with canola oil.

Put a greased 15 cm (6 in) diameter pastry ring into the frying pan and place the pineapple slice in the centre. Spoon or pour pancake batter into the pineapple ring to cover the pineapple, around 1 cm (½ in) in thickness and to reach the edges of the ring. Cook for a couple of minutes or until bubbles break in the centre of the pancake.

Remove the ring, flip the pancake over and cook for a further minute or two until the centre sprigs back when pushed with a finger. Repeat with the remaining pineapple slices and batter.

Serve hot with passionfruit curd and fresh passionfruit pulp.

RASPBERRY BRIOCHE

Serves 8

375 g (13 oz/2½ cups) strong flour
35 g (1¼ oz) caster (superfine) sugar
5 g (¼ oz) dried yeast
5 eggs
pinch of salt
185 g (6½ oz) cold unsalted butter,
  diced
80 g (2¾ oz) whole frozen
  raspberries

A bit of baking to add to your repertoire! This light, fluffy and yeasty loaf of deliciousness has the surprise inclusion of frozen raspberries, which permeate the dough throughout, leaving a taste explosion.

This loaf is perfect to use for my eggy bread recipe on page 127, as the light air bubbles in the dough are ideal for soaking up all of that delicious egg mixture and retaining it throughout cooking, so it stays nice and moist once caramelised.

Place the flour, sugar, dried yeast and eggs in a freestanding electric mixer fitted with the dough hook. Mix on low speed for 10 minutes before adding the salt. Mix for a further 5 minutes.

Add the cold diced butter, one cube at a time, mixing well after each addition. The dough should be smooth, shiny and elastic.

Transfer the dough to a lightly floured bowl and cover with a damp cloth. Leave the dough to prove in a warm spot for 45 minutes or until the dough has doubled in size.

Preheat the oven to 180°C (350°F) and spray a 28 x 13 x 6.5 cm (11 x 5 x 2½ in) loaf (bar) tin then line it with baking paper and spray with canola oil.

Take the dough out of the bowl and place it on a floured work surface. Lightly flour the top of the dough and use your hands to knock the dough into a flat rectangular shape about 30 x 20 cm (12 x 8 in).

Scatter the raspberries evenly over the dough and fold the dough over itself from right to left and press down firmly with your hands.

Roll the brioche dough to fit neatly into the loaf tin. Spray the surface of the dough with canola oil and lay a sheet of plastic wrap loosely over the top to prevent a skin from forming.

Leave the dough to prove in a warm spot for 45 minutes (or until well risen) before baking for around 30–35 minutes in the oven.

Remove the loaf from the oven once it is cooked and leave to cool in the tin until just warm then serve.

RASPBERRY BRIOCHE EGGY BREAD WITH PEANUT BRITTLE ICE CREAM

Serves 4

COMPONENTS
> Peanut brittle ice cream
> Raspberry brioche eggy bread

Truth is, if you had this every day for breakfast you probably wouldn't last very long, but every now and again this is a treat that's too good to miss out on. Use store-bought bread or brioche if you don't have the time to make the recipe on page 124, but make mine if you can as the sharp raspberry inclusion provides a welcome contrast to the sweetness of this dish.

PEANUT BRITTLE ICE CREAM

200 g (7 oz) peanut brittle
400 g (14 oz) Vanilla ice cream
  (see page 173)

In a blender or food processor, blitz the brittle into a coarse crumb.

Scoop the ice cream into the crumb and roll to cover. Set aside in the freezer.

RASPBERRY BRIOCHE EGGY BREAD

½ loaf Raspberry brioche (page 124)
300 ml (10 fl oz) full-cream
  (whole) milk
3 eggs
pinch of salt
130 g (4½ oz) caster (superfine)
  sugar
60 g (2 oz) unsalted butter

Cut the crusts off the brioche and slice it 2 cm (¾ in) thick. Trim the slices to neat rectangles or squares. Place the slices in a sealed container in the refrigerator for a few hours.

Mix the milk, eggs, salt and 30 g (1 oz) of the sugar together well, then strain the mixture into a jug.

Place the brioche slices into a shallow dish and pour over the custard mix. Place in the refrigerator for a minimum of 2 hours – but overnight is great. Flip each slice after an hour or so to get maximum coverage.

Next morning take the slices and place them on a wire rack over a tray to catch the drips. Leave for 20 minutes.

Heat the remaining sugar in a non-stick frying pan over medium heat until the sugar has just melted and is starting to turn a golden brown colour. Reduce the heat to low and add the butter, swirling it around the pan. Add the slices of brioche to the pan and cook them for a couple of minutes until brown and caramelised. Flip them using a fish slice and cook for the same amount of time on the other side.

Remove the slices of brioche from the pan and drain on paper towel.

TO SERVE

fresh raspberries

Serve the eggy bread with the ice cream and some fresh raspberries.

HONEY MADELEINES

Makes 24 madeleines

COMPONENTS
> Honey syrup
> Madeleines

There really is nothing better than these madeleines when they come out of the oven. They're so easy to make and you can get ahead with preparation right up until baking stage. Just leave the tray filled and unbaked in the refrigerator, then pop them in the oven before you take the coffee or tea order from your guests.

Vanessa and Mat from Rooftop Honey are friends who look after my Sweet Studio beehives, and the honey produced in my suburb of South Yarra is amazing. I recommend using a local honey where you can. Try farmers' markets.

HONEY SYRUP

150 ml (5 fl oz) honey
100 ml (3½ fl oz) water
finely grated zest ½ lemon

To make the honey syrup, bring all the ingredients to the boil in a small saucepan over medium heat. Turn off the heat and leave the mixture to infuse for 30 minutes before straining the syrup into a jug.

MADELEINES

90 g (3 oz) unsalted butter
4 eggs
150 g (5½ oz) caster (superfine)
  sugar
20 g (¾ oz) soft light brown sugar
30 g (1 oz) honey
pinch of salt
180 g (6½ oz) plain (all-purpose)
  flour
5 g (¼ oz) baking powder

In a small saucepan over medium heat, cook the butter to a light nutty brown colour, whisking occasionally. Remove the pan from the heat and strain the butter into a small bowl.

Using an electric mixer or whisk, beat the eggs, sugars, honey and salt. Continue to whisk until the mixture becomes pale and doubles in volume.

Sift the flour with the baking powder and gently fold this into the batter, followed by the butter. Rest the batter for a minimum of 2 hours in the refrigerator.

Preheat the oven to 190°C (375°F) and brush a silicone or non-stick madeleine tray.

Remove the batter from the refrigerator and spoon or pipe it into the moulds. Bake for 15–18 minutes or until golden. The sponge should spring back when pushed lightly with the tip of your finger.

TO SERVE

Brush lightly with the honey syrup and serve immediately.

> TIP: This batter works best if you make it the day prior to baking.

DOUGHNUTS

Makes 10

COMPONENTS
> Doughnut dough
> Salted caramel cream (see page 23)
> Caramelised popcorn (page 167)

Doughnuts! They are everywhere and they are easier to make than you might think. However, you'll need a deep-fryer (or a large pan filled with oil) and that means ... beware!

There are endless ways you can pimp up your doughnuts and this is just one idea. You can experiment with fillings and garnishes or even flavour the sugar the doughnuts are rolled in. This combo is delicious but I prefer good old raspberry jam with mine – I am a little bit old school like that.

Have fun and enjoy every last mouthful.

DOUGHNUT DOUGH

250 g (9 oz/1⅔ cups) plain
  (all-purpose) flour
100 g (3½ oz) unsalted butter
3 eggs
5 g (¼ oz) dried yeast
15 g (½ oz) caster (superfine) sugar,
  plus extra for rolling
50 ml (1¾ fl oz) full-cream
  (whole) milk
pinch of salt

Place the flour, butter, eggs, dried yeast, sugar and milk in a freestanding electric mixer fitted with the dough hook. Mix the ingredients well for 8 minutes on low–medium speed. Add the salt and continue to mix for another 5 minutes.

Cover the bowl with a damp tea towel (dish towel) and leave the dough to prove in a warm place for up to an hour or until doubled in size.

Knock the dough back with floured hands then remove the dough from the bowl and transfer it to a liberally floured work surface.

Divide the dough into 10 equal-sized pieces (around 50–55 g/1¾–2 oz each). Shape each piece of dough into a ball and place each ball onto greased squares of baking paper cut to approximately 8 x 8 cm (3¼ x 3¼ in).

Arrange the balls close together on the work surface and lightly spray the dough with canola oil. Rest plastic wrap on top of the doughnuts to prevent them getting a skin. Prove the doughnuts for a further 30–45 minutes or until they have expanded in size.

Half-fill a large saucepan with sunflower oil and heat to a temperature of 165°C (330°F), using a thermometer to accurately check the temperature. (Or use a deep-fryer.) >

Cook a couple of doughnuts at a time by gently picking them up using two opposite corners of the baking paper and dropping the whole thing carefully into the oil. The paper will lift itself away from the doughnut. You can now use tongs to retrieve the paper and discard. Cook the doughnuts for around 4 minutes on each side using a slotted metal spoon to flip them in the oil.

Once cooked, lift the doughnuts from the oil with the slotted spoon and place them on paper towel to absorb any excess oil.

Roll the hot doughnuts in a tray of caster sugar to coat.

ASSEMBLY
Salted caramel cream
Caramelised popcorn

Once the doughnuts have cooled sufficiently, use a sharp paring knife to cut a cavity into one end of each doughnut. Push through into the centre of the doughnut and reverse the knife to use the handle to widen the cavity inside the doughnut.

Fill the doughnut with as much salted caramel cream as you can and serve with caramelised popcorn.

VARIATIONS FOR FILLING

Lemon curd (see page 78)
Honeycomb (page 164)
Raspberry jam (page 52)
Passionfruit curd (see page 221)
Milk or dark chocolate cream (see page 57)
Ice cream

PISTACHIO 'PERSUADERS'

Makes 45–50

190 g (6½ oz) unsalted butter
40 g (1½ oz) caster (superfine) sugar
75 g (2¾ oz) soft light brown sugar
20 g (¾ oz) pistachio paste, sweetened and coloured (optional)
200 g (7 oz/1⅓ cups) plain (all-purpose) flour
20 g (¾ oz) baking powder
100 g (3½ oz/¾ cup) pistachio nuts, coarsely chopped
25 g (1 oz/¼ cup) ground almonds
45 ml (1½ fl oz) full-cream (whole) milk
finely grated zest of 2 lemons
½ drop edible mint essential oil
300 g (10½ oz) white chocolate, melted

There was a TV show a loooong time ago called *The Persuaders* and it starred the super-smooth and super-suave actor, Roger Moore. These biscuits share his qualities and, as such, are named after him. There is always room for one Moore.

If you can't find pistachio paste then you can leave it out, but it does add to the flavour and colour. It can be found in specialist cookware and specialist food shops or online.

Place the butter, the sugars and the pistachio paste in a freestanding electric mixer fitted with the paddle attachment. Slowly beat the mixture on low speed until smooth, ensuring all the lumps of butter are removed. Scrape the inside of the bowl down with a spatula and mix again until smooth.

Sift the flour and baking powder into the bowl. Mix on low speed for 1 minute then add the nuts, milk and lemon zest and mix again. Scrape the side of the bowl to ensure an even mix of ingredients and no lumps.

Transfer the dough to a lightly floured work surface and knead to bring it together with your hands. Roll the dough into a log shape and divide it into three equal-sized pieces of around 300 g (10½ oz) each.

Roll each piece into equal-sized log shapes with a diameter of around 4–5 cm (1½–2 in).

Wrap the logs in plastic wrap and chill them in the freezer for a minimum of 45 minutes.

Preheat the oven to 170°C (340°F) and line a baking tray with baking paper.

Remove the dough from the refrigerator and remove the plastic wrap. Cut the logs into 1 cm (½ in) 'slices' of biscuit, using a sharp knife.

Place the biscuits on the prepared baking tray, evenly spaced apart, and bake them for 14 minutes or until the biscuits are just starting to go brown and they crumble once cooled.

Remove the biscuits from the oven and immediately transfer them, using a palette knife, to a wire rack to cool. >

Stir the mint oil into the chocolate and stir the chocolate until it cools to around 30°C (86°F), using a digital thermometer to accurately check the temperature.

Dip each biscuit completely in the white mint chocolate, using a fork or palette knife, then shake each one to remove any excess chocolate. Lie them flat on a tray lined with baking paper and leave them to set at room temperature before serving.

> TIPS: You can make this dough, roll it out like pastry and chill it before cutting out 7.5 cm (3 in) discs. Bake them as directed in this recipe and use them to sandwich one of the delicious ice creams or parfaits from this book and you'll have your own twist on an ice cream sandwich.

Try using the biscuit dough for a crumble topping. If you don't want to use pistachio paste, you can replace it with another nut paste.

If you don't have a thermometer, melt the chocolate in short high bursts in the microwave on High (100%) until it is runny but feels cool to touch. That will be the right temperature for the chocolate to set on the biscuits. If you are having trouble, pop them in the refrigerator for 20 minutes to finish setting.

Left: Pistachio 'persuaders' (page 133);
right: White and dark chocolate coconut biscuits (page 138)

WHITE AND DARK CHOCOLATE COCONUT BISCUITS

Makes 35

190 g (6½ oz) unsalted butter

110 g (4 oz) caster (superfine) sugar

195 g (7 oz) plain (all-purpose) flour

25 g (1 oz) Dutch (unsweetened) cocoa powder

15 g (½ oz) baking powder

110 g (4 oz) desiccated coconut

45 g (1½ oz) white chocolate, chopped into small pieces

45 ml (1½ fl oz) full-cream (whole) milk

300 g (10½ oz/2 cups) dark chocolate, melted for dipping (see page 142)

I really love chocolate-dipped biscuits. I mean I really, really love chocolate-dipped biscuits. They were a special treat around our house when I was younger. We had lots of biscuits (for tea dipping of course) but the chocolate variety biscuits were a bit fancy.

Biscuit dipping in tea was a special skill I acquired and practised in my childhood. Real pros at the sport could get maximum tea soakage into the biscuit without it crumbling into the cuppa. Chocolate-dipped biscuits, though, are a totally different ball game; with that chocolatey protective covering you need all your wits about you to get the tea soakage to a maximum. Now I make my own dipped biscuits and I luxuriate in the decadence of it all, munching and dipping at will. And you can too if you give these a try.

This is a recipe that has lots of uses such as playing the bread part in my Lamington ice cream sandwiches (page 235). You can use it as a crumble topping or a pie lid, there is no limit really but one of the best and simplest ways is to bake them as a cookie and dip them in chocolate. Ridiculous, pure heaven.

Place the butter and sugar in a freestanding electric mixer fitted with the paddle attachment. Slowly beat the mixture on low speed until smooth, ensuring there are no lumps of butter. Scrape the side of the bowl with a spatula and mix again until smooth.

Sift the flour, cocoa powder and baking powder into a bowl. Mix again on low speed for 1 minute then add the coconut, white chocolate and milk. Mix again and make sure you scrape down the side of the bowl to ensure an even mix of ingredients and no lumps.

Transfer the dough to a lightly floured work surface and bring it together with your hands. Roll the dough into a log shape and divide it into two even pieces of around 350 g (12½ oz) each.

Roll each piece into an equal-sized log shape with a diameter of around 4–5 cm (1½–2 in).

Wrap each log in plastic wrap and store in the refrigerator for a minimum of 45 minutes.

Preheat the oven to 170°C (340°F). Line a baking tray with baking paper.

Remove the dough from the refrigerator and remove the plastic wrap. Cut 5 mm (¼ in) 'slices' of biscuit using a sharp knife.

Place the biscuits on the prepared baking tray, evenly spaced apart, and bake them in the oven for 14 minutes or until they are just starting to go golden brown and are cooked through.

Remove the biscuits from the oven and immediately transfer them, using a palette knife, to a wire rack to cool down.

Prepare the chocolate for dipping.

Dip each biscuit completely in the dark chocolate, using a fork or palette knife, and shake each one to remove any excess chocolate before lying them flat on a tray lined with baking paper. Leave them to set at room temperature then serve.

> TIP: If you don't have a thermometer, just melt the chocolate in short bursts on High (100%) in the microwave until it is runny but feels cool to the touch. That will be the right temperature for the chocolate to set on the biscuits. If you are having trouble, pop them in the refrigerator for 20 minutes to finish setting.

Sweet Essentials

CHOCOLATE

Chocolate! It's one of my all-time favourite ingredients and it shows because chocolate features heavily in my creations. It is handy to know a few tricks and tips, though, to help you get the most out of this luxurious ingredient and make the best possible cakes and desserts. I use couverture chocolate, which is a chocolate that contains more cocoa butter than regular chocolate. It produces a better finish on any of my sweet recipes that contain chocolate as it creates great snap and shine. Couverture chocolate is widely available in specialist food ingredient shops or online and can be found in some supermarkets these days, too.

There are three main types of couverture – dark, milk and white couverture – and these all have varying levels of sweetness, cocoa solids, cocoa butter and milk inclusions. I love all three chocolates equally and mostly use dark chocolate on its own. I use milk chocolate for real crowd-pleasing desserts and I tend to use white in conjunction with other flavours or infusions. White chocolate is sweeter so it works well with stronger or more tangy fruits or flavours.

DIFFERENT TYPES AND QUALITY OF CHOCOLATE

The better quality chocolate that you use is obviously going to have a positive effect on your work. Some of the lesser and cheaper brands of chocolate can contain lots of sugar and even vegetable oil, so try to buy the best you can afford. Of course, because of the price of this ingredient, it is advisable that you concentrate when cooking with chocolate. Mistakes are costly.

I use a variety of chocolates depending on what is available to me, but the most common brands I use are Callebaut and Cacao Barry. I use a good-quality white and milk chocolate and I like to use dark chocolate with cocoa solids ranging from 50 to 65 per cent. I always try to use buttons for ease of melting.

WORKING WITH CHOCOLATE

When you are doing anything chocolate-related, always make sure you are working in a cool environment, I prefer an air-conditioned room set to 18°C (64°F) for most of my chocolate work. Also ensure your work surfaces and equipment, such as bowls, palette knives and spatulas are meticulously clean. Invest in a digital thermometer so you can check temperatures accurately and store unused chocolate in sealed plastic containers in the pantry.

MELTING CHOCOLATE

This book calls for quite a bit of chocolate melting and, although it may seem a simple task, it is worth doing it the right way to make sure you get the best results.

The most commonly taught method of melting chocolate is to place the chocolate in a bowl and heat it over a double boiler (a bowl set over a saucepan of simmering water). This works well enough, but it is not my preferred method due to a couple of factors. One is that it is easy to overheat the chocolate because the heat underneath the bowl can be quite harsh. Another drawback is the fact that steam escapes from the side of the bowl and this can end up in your chocolate, which could seize the mixture – plus you can burn yourself from the steam when you lift the bowl of chocolate from the pan.

I prefer to use the microwave to melt all of my chocolate under 2 kg (4 lb 6 oz) in quantity as I find it easier to control and there is no need for any unwanted water. To do this correctly, you need to follow these simple steps. First choose an adequately sized, microwave-safe bowl. Make sure the bowl is clean. Add the chocolate, either in button form or chopped into small pieces if using a block. Heat the chocolate on High (100%) speed for short bursts at a time. Remember the microwave can burn your chocolate if you are not careful. I like to heat the chocolate in bursts of up to 30 seconds at a time. I stir my chocolate in between each burst and I generally heat the chocolate to 40–45°C (104–113°F). This is the best temperature for chocolate to be melted to, and it is from here that it can be successfully tempered or added to mixes.

Always stir after each burst of heat to ensure an even temperature throughout. Also, use a digital thermometer to accurately check temperatures. For every recipe in this book that calls for melted chocolate, I recommend using the microwave method.

TEMPERING CHOCOLATE

This is where things get a little tricky – but not too much so don't worry. Once the chocolate has been melted, it is now perfect for adding to mixes or brushing onto items. However, if you want to make some simple decorations or dip biscuits in chocolate, you will have to adjust the temperature of the chocolate to allow it to crystallise, which will result in it getting a good shine and prevent it from melting too quickly on the product.

You need to bring the temperature of the melted chocolate down from 45°C (113°F) to 28°C (82°F). You can do this by adding unmelted chocolate buttons a few at a time to the hot, melted chocolate and stirring them in. The temperature of the chocolate will automatically drop – you must keep stirring and scraping the side of the bowl with a silicone spatula. Now you have to bring the temperature back up to 31°C (88°F), your working temperature. The two best ways of bringing the temperature back up are to heat the bowl of chocolate in the microwave on High (100%) in very short bursts or to add warm melted chocolate to your bowl and stir until the temperature rises. The chocolate is now ready for you to use for decorations and dipping.

TEMPERING CHOCOLATE AND MAKING CURLS

  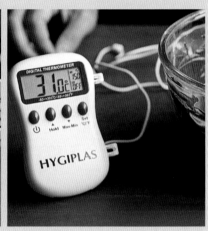

1 Once you have melted the chocolate, you need to bring the temperature down so the chocolate crystallises.

2 The temperature of the chocolate needs to reach 28°C (82°F).

3 Then it is time to bring that temperature back up to 31°C (88°F), which will be your working temperature.

DIPPING IN CHOCOLATE

Biscuits, fudge and wagon wheels (see my recipe on page 147) can all be dipped in tempered milk, white and dark chocolate. All you need to do is prepare the chocolate (as above) then pour it into a deep and narrow bowl and line a tray with baking paper. Dip the biscuits or wagon wheels entirely in the chocolate and lift them out with a spatula or fork. Shake off any excess chocolate and gently place the biscuits or wagon wheels onto the prepared baking tray. You can add any garnishing sprinkles now while the chocolate is still tacky. Place the dipped biscuits or wheels into the refrigerator for 5 minutes to set the chocolate.

CHOCOLATE CURLS

These are an easy and cute little garnish, which are very handy to have on hand for jazzing up desserts, cakes and tarts, such as my Chocolate and salted caramel tarts with caramelised hazelnuts (page 97).

4 Prepare the chocolate for tempering (see opposite) and pour a small amount onto a flat work surface.

5 Spread the chocolate out neatly, using a palette knife. Leave to set slightly but it should still be a little tacky.

6 Take a small sharp paring knife and cut vertical strips in the chocolate, about 2–3 cm (¾–1¼ in) in width.

7 Take a flexible metal scraper and start to push the edge into the now-set chocolate to form rolls or curls in the chocolate.

8 Repeat until you have enough curls. Allow them to set on the work surface for 10 minutes before picking them up with the end of the scraper.

9 Store the chocolate curls in a sealed plastic container until needed. These can be made well in advance of when you need them.

CHOCOLATE FLAKES

These are similar to curls but there is no prior cutting with the knife. This means you get longer shavings that can be used as 'flake' pieces. Pour some chocolate on a flat work surface. Spread it out with a palette knife. Take a flexible metal scraper and start to push the edge into the set chocolate to form the flakes. Repeat until you have enough pieces. Allow them to set on the work surface for 10 minutes before picking them up with the end of the scraper and storing them in a sealed plastic container. These can be made well in advance of when you actually need them. You can also shave finer pieces of chocolate to use for shavings, which are another great garnish.

CANNELÉ

Makes 24

500 ml (17 fl oz/2 cups) full-cream
  (whole) milk
50 g (1¾ oz) unsalted butter
1 vanilla bean, seeds scraped
2 eggs, lightly beaten
2 egg yolks, lightly beaten
250 g (9 oz/2 cups) icing
  (confectioners') sugar, sifted
125 g (4½ oz) plain (all-purpose)
  flour
200 g (7 oz) clarified butter (ghee)
200 g (7 oz) melted beeswax
1 tablespoon dark rum
finely grated zest of 1 lemon

These are absolutely delicious and a real talking point with the addition of the beeswax. I used to make these when I was pastry chef at Vue de Monde in Melbourne and they were a big hit with the diners there. The beeswax used to line the moulds adds a unique flavour profile and helps with the shine. Make sure you bake these thoroughly to ensure they have a crispy dark exterior and soft chewy interior.

Put the milk, butter and vanilla seeds in a saucepan over medium heat and bring to the boil. Set aside and keep warm.

Whisk the eggs and egg yolks together.

Sift the icing sugar and flour into a mixing bowl. Add the eggs and stir gently with a fork.

Pour the warm milk mixture into the bowl and mix with a fork or whisk to eradicate any lumps. Try not to beat too much air into the batter at this stage.

Strain the mixture into a bowl and rest in the refrigerator for a minimum of 24 hours and for up to 2 days.

Prepare your cannelé moulds by heating them in a warm oven.

Combine the clarified butter with the melted beeswax in a bowl.

Pour the butter–wax mixture into each warmed cannelé mould and fill it up to the lip. Pour any excess mixture back into the butter–wax. Allow the moulds to cool naturally on a wire rack, open side down, to drip free. Prepare 24 moulds and set aside.

Preheat the oven to 200°C (400°F).

Pour the rested batter halfway up the moulds and place them on a baking tray.

Bake the cannelé for 30 minutes before turning the tray around and cooking for a further 15 minutes until dark brown.

Turn the cannelé out while they are warm and eat on the day.

> TIP: You can use just melted and clarified butter if you cannot source beeswax. Cannelé moulds have traditionally been expensive, but you can now find fairly inexpensive cannelé tray moulds that work very well.

EXPLOSIVE RASPBERRY WAGON WHEELS

Makes 12

COMPONENTS
> Chocolate sablé
> Marshmallow

These are like little individual milk chocolate time machines that can transport you instantly back to your childhood. I grew up eating Wagon Wheels back in the UK so was surprised and happy to find them here in Australia when I moved over many years ago. It seems kids here were enjoying them just as much as me when I was on the other side of the world.

I make hundreds of these a week in my store and they are super popular. My customers are always asking me for the recipe, so now you too can make your own. These are great fun to make with the kids and they really pack an explosive punch, with the addition of the chocolate-coated popping candy. This component is easily found online or in specialist food ingredient shops.

Now I might eat a wagon wheel and go back and tell my past self how fun it would be to write a book called *Lamingtons & Lemon Tart*, it might inspire me sooner. Or perhaps I have already? I need a chair, I've confused myself.

CHOCOLATE SABLÉ

250 g (9 oz/1⅓ cups) plain (all-purpose) flour, sifted
30 g (1 oz/¼ cup) Dutch (unsweetened) cocoa powder, sifted
90 g (3 oz/¾ cup) icing (confectioners') sugar, sifted
pinch of salt
135 g (5 oz) cold unsalted butter, diced
1 egg
1 egg yolk

Place the flour, cocoa powder, icing sugar and salt in a freestanding electric mixer fitted with the paddle attachment. Turn the machine to low speed, add the butter and mix until you have a fine sandy texture.

Add the egg and egg yolk and mix again until the dough starts to come together. Turn it out onto a lightly floured work surface and knead it together briefly with your hands.

Form a square shape with the dough and flatten it onto a large piece of plastic wrap. Cover the dough completely with the wrap then chill and rest it in the refrigerator for 45 minutes.

Remove the dough from the refrigerator and cut it into two equal pieces.

Roll the first piece of dough out, in between two sheets of baking paper, to achieve a thickness of 1–2 mm (¹⁄₁₆–⅛ in). Repeat with the second piece of dough then chill and rest the rolled pastry in the refrigerator, still between the sheets of baking paper, for 20 minutes.

Preheat the oven to 170°C (340°F) and line two baking trays with baking paper. >

<

Remove the sheets of pastry from the refrigerator and pull off the top sheet of baking paper. Using a 7 cm (2¾ in) round pastry cutter, cut out 24 discs from the two sheets of pastry.

Place the discs on the prepared baking trays and bake them in the oven for 10–12 minutes or until crisp to touch and cooked through.

Remove from the oven and allow the discs to cool on the trays.

MARSHMALLOW

4 egg whites
400 g (14 oz/1¾ cups) caster (superfine) sugar
1 tablespoon liquid glucose
10 gold-strength gelatine leaves (20 g/¾ oz), soaked and drained (see page 33)
2 teaspoons freeze-dried raspberry powder (optional)

Place the egg whites in a freestanding electric mixer on low speed and start to whisk slowly.

Place 150 ml (5 fl oz) water, the caster sugar and glucose in a small saucepan over medium heat. Stir gently to dissolve the sugar and bring it to the boil.

Once the syrup comes to the boil, turn the mixer with the egg whites to medium speed.

Cook the syrup to 125°C (257°F), using a digital or sugar thermometer to check the temperature accurately.

Slowly trickle the syrup down one side of the bowl with the whisking egg whites, in a constant stream, ensuring the syrup doesn't touch the whisk.

Melt the gelatine in the still-hot saucepan and add it to the bowl. Whisk well until the mixture starts to cool and thicken then add the freeze-dried raspberry powder, if using.

Transfer the mixture to a piping (icing) bag fitted with a large plain nozzle.

> TIP: Left-over marshmallow can be piped into bulbs on a lightly greased baking tray for use as a garnish or extra component for any number of other desserts.

ASSEMBLY

60 g (2 oz) raspberry jam (see the recipe on page 52 if you'd like to make your own)
melted milk chocolate
chocolate-coated popping candy
freeze-dried raspberries

Place 12 cooked chocolate sablé bases on a tray or work surface, evenly spaced apart. Reserve another 12 cooked chocolate sablé discs to the side.

Place a teaspoon of raspberry jam in the centre of each of the 12 discs.

Pipe about 60 g (2 oz) of marshmallow into the centre of each disc over the jam and to the edge of each disc.

Top the marshmallow with a reserved cooked chocolate sablé disc and gently push down to level.

Finish the 12 wheels and reserve for 4 hours, uncovered, at room temperature.

Line a tray with baking paper and prepare the milk chocolate. (See page 142 for instructions on tempering and dipping in chocolate.)

Dip a wheel in the melted milk chocolate and lift it out with a spatula. Shake off the excess chocolate and gently place the wheel back on the prepared baking tray. Sprinkle some chocolate-coated popping candy and freeze-dried raspberries onto the tacky chocolate.

Complete all 12 wagon wheels and leave them to set at room temperature for 30 minutes.

Place the wheels in the refrigerator for 5 minutes to set the chocolate well.

The wheels are ready to be served immediately or boxed for gifts. They are good for a few weeks if stored in a sealed container, in or out of the refrigerator.

VARIATIONS

You're not limited to this flavour combination – try different chocolates, marshmallows or jams. You could switch the jam for orange marmalade, make an orange marshmallow (flavouring with orange zest instead of raspberry powder) or dip them in dark chocolate with edible orange oil for a jaffa orange wagon wheel.

DATE, ORANGE AND CHOCOLATE BUTTERMILK SCONES

Makes 12–16

500 g (1 lb 2 oz/3⅓ cups) plain (all-purpose) flour
30 g (1 oz) baking powder
125 g (4½ oz) caster (superfine) sugar
pinch of salt
125 g (4½ oz) unsalted butter
200 ml (7 fl oz) buttermilk
175 g (6 oz) pitted dates, chopped
finely grated zest of 1 orange
85 g (3 oz) dark chocolate, roughly chopped
egg wash (1 egg + splash milk + pinch of salt)

Who doesn't love a warm scone with butter? If you know someone like this then be wary, they are not to be trusted. These scones are delicious served warm with organic fruit preserves and clotted cream. Sliced strawberries and crème fraîche can be used for a lighter alternative.

Sift the flour and baking powder together in a mixing bowl and add the sugar and salt.

Using your fingertips, or a freestanding electric mixer fitted with the paddle attachment, crumble the ingredients until you have a light sandy texture.

Add the buttermilk, dates, orange zest and chocolate. Knead until a dough forms. Cover the dough with plastic wrap and leave to rest at room temperature for 15 minutes.

Roll out the dough on a lightly floured work surface to a thickness of 3 cm (1¼ in).

Preheat the oven to 180°C (350°F). Line a baking tray with silicone paper or baking paper.

Using a 5 cm (2 in) round cutter, cut out the scones. Repeat this process twice with the trimmings. Discard any left-over trimmings.

Place the scones on the prepared baking tray. Using a pastry brush, glaze the tops of the scones neatly with the egg wash. Bake for 12–15 minutes until they are baked through with a golden-brown glaze. Leave to cool for 10 minutes before serving.

VARIATION

You can try other variations by combining dry goods with the finished dough before cutting, such as sultanas (golden raisins), chocolate chips, dried apricots, other citrus zests and nuts.

CHOCOLATE, ALMOND AND CRANBERRY FUDGE FINGERS

Makes 18

240 g (8½ oz) caster (superfine) sugar
80 g (2¾ oz) liquid glucose
100 ml (3½ fl oz) thickened (whipping) cream
700 g (1 lb 9 oz/4⅔ cups) milk chocolate, roughly chopped
15 g (½ oz) unsalted butter
pinch of salt
75 g (2¾ oz) whole blanched almonds, toasted and chopped
75 g (2¾ oz) dried cranberries, chopped

Chewy, nutty and chocolatey, these are really easy to make and can satisfy that afternoon sweet craving. They also make lovely gifts.

Line a 28 x 18 x 3.5 cm (11 x 7 x 1½ in) non-stick baking tin with greased baking paper to fit the base exactly.

Place the sugar, glucose and cream in a large heavy-based saucepan over medium heat. (I like to use a cast-iron pan, but you can use stainless steel.)

Bring the mixture to the boil, stirring regularly with a wooden spoon or heat-resistant spatula. Cook the mixture to a temperature of 121°C (250°F), using a digital or sugar thermometer to accurately check the temperature.

Once the temperature has been reached, remove the saucepan from the heat and add 200 g (7 oz) of the milk chocolate, the butter, salt, nuts and fruit to the pan. Stir carefully with a wooden spoon to bring the mixture together.

Pour the fudge into the prepared tin and flatten it down and into the corners with a spatula.

Leave the fudge to cool overnight before running a small knife around the edge of the tin to loosen. Turn the fudge out onto a chopping board and remove the paper.

Use a sharp knife to cut the fudge in half lengthways and then cut each strip into 2 cm (¾ in) widths. You will yield around 18 fingers.

Prepare the remaining milk chocolate for dipping (see page 142). Dip each finger in the chocolate and place it on a tray lined with baking paper. Repeat with the remaining fingers. Leave the fingers to cool before placing them in the refrigerator for 20 minutes. Store in a sealed container in the pantry for up to 3 months.

BABAS WITH NECTARINES POACHED IN GINGER SYRUP

Makes 8

COMPONENTS
> Babas
> Nectarines poached in
  ginger syrup

The smells and flavours from this dish are ridiculously good.

This is such a beautiful way to prepare the nectarines. Using the soaking liquid to gently remove the skins makes the fruit taste amazing and also adds to the flavour of the syrup.

I used nectarines as they were bang in season when writing this, but it would not be too much of a problem if they were not available and you used an apricot, peach, plum or even a pear.

BABAS

40 ml (1¼ fl oz) full-cream (whole) milk
200 g (7 oz/1⅓ cups) strong flour
15 g (½ oz) sugar
7 g (¼ oz) dried yeast
3 eggs
pinch of salt
80 g (2¾ oz) unsalted butter, softened, plus extra for greasing

Brush the insides of eight 5 cm (2 in) wide x 5 cm (2 in) deep non-stick dariole moulds with softened butter and place the moulds in the refrigerator for the butter to harden.

Place the flour, sugar, dried yeast and eggs in a freestanding electric mixer fitted with the dough hook. Mix for 8 minutes on low speed before adding the salt. Mix for a further 5 minutes.

Cover the bowl with a damp cloth and prove the dough somewhere warm until it has doubled in size.

Place the bowl back on the mixer and reattach the dough hook. Mix well and gradually incorporate the softened butter until it has all been incorporated and the dough is smooth and elastic.

Again cover the bowl with a damp cloth and prove the dough somewhere warm until it has doubled in size.

Knock back the dough and transfer it to a piping (icing) bag. Cut a 1 cm (½ in) hole at the end of the bag and pipe the dough halfway up each dariole mould. Use scissors to snip off the dough, as it is very elastic.

Lightly spray the tops of the babas with canola oil and gently cover them with plastic wrap.

Preheat the oven to 200°C (400°F).

Place the babas in a warm place and allow them to prove until doubled in size. This should take 45 minutes or so. Remove the plastic wrap and bake for 12–14 minutes until golden brown and firm to the touch.

Remove the babas from the oven, unmould onto a wire rack and allow them to cool. >

NECTARINES POACHED IN GINGER SYRUP

300 ml (10 fl oz) Stone's ginger
  wine
280 g (10 oz) caster (superfine)
  sugar
2 vanilla beans, seeds scraped
finely grated zest of 2 oranges
20 g (¾ oz) fresh ginger, peeled
  and grated
4 ripe nectarines, loose-stone
  variety

Place the ginger wine, 400 ml (13½ fl oz) water, the sugar, vanilla, orange zest and ginger in a saucepan over medium heat and bring to the boil. Stir to dissolve the sugar.

Cut the nectarines in half and remove the stones. Add the fruit to the pan and simmer for 5 minutes before turning the heat off. Leave to infuse for 30 minutes before removing the fruit. The nectarine skins should now peel away easily from the fruit. Discard the skins and reserve the fruit.

Reheat the syrup to a boil. Turn the heat off and add the babas to the syrup, two at a time, and use a spoon to coat and soak the babas. Soak for a few minutes then transfer them to a wire rack set over a tray to catch any drips. Reserve the syrup for serving.

TO SERVE

thickened (whipping) cream

Serve the soaked babas with the poached nectarines, extra ginger syrup and cream on the side.

CHOCOLATE AND BANANA TOASTIES WITH PEANUT BUTTER CARAMEL

Makes 4

COMPONENTS
> Chocolate cream
> Peanut butter caramel
> Brioche or bread loaf

I've always wanted to write a cookbook devoted to toasted sandwiches. It's on the bucket list along with 'open my own pastry shop' (tick) and score a part in *Neighbours* (tick – yes really! Episode 7209).

I think my favourite food is toast or sandwiches – combine the two and I'm in heaven. I love savoury toasties with grilled cheese and onion and a splash of Worcestershire, but having a sweet tooth means I also equally love sandwiches oozing with chocolate or caramel or both, then dusted liberally with icing (confectioners') sugar.

Sure, these are not the healthiest, but I reckon once in a while never hurt anyone? It pays to make your own brioche or bread if you have the time, but bread from the local bakery is fine.

Make a stack of these and freeze them individually. You can cook from chilled or frozen, so they are super-easy to get ready. There is also no law preventing you eating this with ice cream. Try one of the flavours from this book. Banana (see page 179), nut butter (see page 189) or vanilla (see page 173) would be perfect.

You crack on with these and I'll get back to that other book … roasted pear, gorgonzola and walnut toastie anyone?

CHOCOLATE CREAM

110 g (4 oz) dark chocolate, roughly chopped
125 ml (4 fl oz/½ cup) thickened (whipping) cream
1 tablespoon liquid glucose
25 g (1 oz) unsalted butter, at room temperature

Put the chocolate in a bowl.

Put the cream and liquid glucose in a saucepan over medium heat and bring to the boil. Remove the pan from the heat and pour the hot mixture over the chocolate.

Leave it to stand for 30 seconds before adding the butter and stirring it with a silicone spatula until you have a smooth and shiny cream.

Cover the surface of the cream with plastic wrap and leave to cool at room temperature for a couple of hours. >

PEANUT BUTTER CARAMEL

150 ml (5 fl oz) thickened
  (whipping) cream
60 g (2 oz) peanut butter, smooth
  or crunchy
100 g (3½ oz) caster (superfine)
  sugar

Put the cream in a saucepan over medium heat and bring to the boil. Remove from the heat and whisk in the peanut butter. Set aside.

Place a separate large saucepan over medium heat for a minute to get hot. Gradually add the sugar to the pan in three stages. Stir each batch with a wooden spoon or heat-resistant spatula to dissolve the sugar and cook it to a deep amber colour before adding the next batch.

Once all the sugar is in and you have a golden caramel, add half the scalded peanut butter cream. BE CAREFUL! This mixture will expand furiously and the steam is extremely hot. Whisk the mixture and gradually add the remaining cream until it is all in.

Remove from the heat and serve immediately or leave to cool a little to thicken up.

> TIP: This sauce can be made in larger batches or in advance and stored in the refrigerator. Just melt it in a saucepan over medium–low heat or in a microwave to warm it up before serving.

ASSEMBLY

eight 1 cm (½ in) slices brioche or
  good-quality white bread, any
  shape but square does work well
smoked salt flakes to sprinkle
1 banana, cut into 5 mm (¼ in) slices
unsalted butter, softened
icing (confectioners') sugar for
  dusting

Lay all of the brioche or bread slices on a work surface or chopping board and liberally spread the chocolate cream on each slice. Use a knife or palette knife to spread the cream to just inside the edges of the slices and make sure it is nice and thick. Sprinkle a few smoked salt flakes on top.

Arrange the slices of banana on four of the slices and top these slices with the remaining four slices of bread. Press down gently and then spread the top with some softened unsalted butter.

Flip each sandwich, butter side down, on a sheet of plastic wrap and butter the new top side of the sandwich. Close the plastic wrap and store in the refrigerator for a minimum of 2 hours.

Heat a sandwich press or frying pan. Remove the sandwich/es from the refrigerator and open the plastic wrap. Dust each side of the sandwich with icing sugar and place the sandwich in the press or frying pan. Cook for a couple of minutes (on each side if using a frying pan) or until the brioche is golden brown and crispy and you can see chocolate sauce starting to ooze out.

Remove the sandwich from the press or pan and leave to sit for a minute. Cut the sandwich in half and arrange on a plate with more icing sugar and some peanut butter caramel.

Eat, enjoy, sleep, repeat.

CHOCOLATE MILK

Serves 4

Perfect for children and adults alike, this recipe can provide an energy boost or cool relief on a hot day, or you can drink it hot to warm you up in the afternoon or evening in winter.

This is easy to whip up once you have the base chocolate blocks in the freezer. The base blocks are simple to prepare and they can be infused with endless flavours. Then fresh chocolate milk is never a moment or two away. Just boil some milk, add the chocolate blocks and emulsify in a stand blender or use a hand-held blender.

FROZEN CHOCOLATE MILK BLOCKS

175 g (6 oz) dark chocolate, roughly chopped
100 g (3½ oz) milk chocolate, chopped
100 ml (3½ fl oz) thickened (whipping) cream
100 ml (3½ fl oz) full-cream (whole) milk
pinch of salt

Combine the chocolates in a microwave-safe bowl and gently melt them together in the microwave.

Place the cream, milk and salt in a saucepan over medium heat and bring to a simmer.

Pour the hot cream mixture over the chocolate mixture and stir gently, from the middle of the bowl to the outside, using a silicone spatula. Stir until the chocolate is fully melted and continue to mix until you have a shiny emulsion.

Pour this mixture into ice cube trays or similar and freeze the cubes of chocolate until needed.

VARIATIONS

The cream and milk can be infused with a variety of flavours. Bring the cream and milk to a simmer with spices and/or citrus zests or teas. Strain the infusions and re-boil to proceed with the recipe.

MY FAVOURITE INFUSIONS

Orange zest and star anise
Coffee and fennel seeds
Green tea and kaffir lime
Jasmine tea and lemon
Chilli >

<

SAMPLE RECIPE: Put 100 ml (3½ fl oz) full-cream (whole) milk and 100 ml (3½ fl oz) thickened (whipping) cream in a saucepan over medium heat and bring to the boil. Remove from the heat, add 10 g (¼ oz) Earl Grey tea leaves, stir and infuse for 5 minutes. Strain.

> TIP: Don't infuse tea for too long or it can result in bitterness. I recommend infusing milk and cream with more tea than you would use to make a drink but infuse for a maximum of 5 minutes.

CHOCOLATE MILK DRINK FORMULATION

400 g (14 oz) frozen chocolate
  blocks
800 ml (27 fl oz) full-cream
  (whole) milk

Place the frozen chocolate blocks in a stand blender, or a tall cylindrical container if you are using a hand-held blender.

Put the milk in a saucepan over medium heat and bring to the boil. Pour it over the chocolate blocks. Carefully blend and emulsify the two ingredients together.

Remove the chocolate milk from the blender and cool or reheat as required. Serve immediately in glasses, mugs or small milk bottles.

> TIP: To reheat the milk, use a microwave or saucepan and heat it to above 80°C (176°F). Serve with some left-over raspberry marshmallow bulbs from the Explosive raspberry wagon wheels (page 147).

QUICK, THICK AND NAUGHTY HOT CHOCOLATE

Serves 4

250 g (9 oz) dark chocolate,
  roughly chopped
125 ml (4 fl oz/½ cup) thickened
  (whipping) cream
375 ml (12 ½ fl oz/1½ cups) full-
  cream (whole) milk
pinch of salt

As a bonus here's my very naughty thick hot chocolate for those days when you really need a chocolate boost.

Put the chocolate in a bowl.

Place the cream, milk and salt in a saucepan over medium–low heat and bring to a simmer. Pour around one-quarter of the mixture over the chocolate and stir to melt.

Add the remaining cream mixture and stir. Return the mixture to the pan and heat to 85°C (185°F), using a sugar or digital thermometer for accuracy. Serve hot and topped with whipped cream to make it extra naughty.

> TIP: This is even more decadent with marshmallows left over and piped from the Explosive raspberry wagon wheels (page 147).

CHOCOLATE-COATED CARAMELISED HAZELNUTS

Makes lots

40 g (1½ oz) caster (superfine) sugar
75 g (2¾ oz) whole shelled hazelnuts
100 g (3½ oz) dark chocolate, melted
Dutch (unsweetened) cocoa powder for dusting

These are incredibly delicious, crunchy and decadent. I use them in the book to garnish the Chocolate and salted caramel tarts with caramelised hazelnuts (page 97), but they can be used as a garnish for any dessert or tart. They also make a great gift for someone as they can be bagged up nicely with a ribbon.

Place the sugar, 25 ml (¾ fl oz) water and the hazelnuts in a saucepan over low heat and start to heat gently. Stir gently but constantly over the heat. The water will boil and begin to evaporate then the nuts will crystallise heavily. Continue to cook and stir past that stage then the nuts will start to gain an even caramel coating. Don't cook the nuts and sugar too far – a golden colour caramel is perfect.

Using a fork, flick the nuts onto a baking tray lined with baking paper. Ensure no two nuts are touching as they will stick together once cold. If the pan loses heat too quickly and the nuts become tricky to extract, simply place the pan back over low heat to warm them through.

Once all the nuts are removed from the pan, allow them to cool.

Place a couple of nuts at a time into the melted dark chocolate, coat and remove them with a fork making sure you tap away any excess chocolate. Immediately roll the nuts in cocoa powder.

Once the nuts are all coated, remove them from the cocoa powder and store them in a sealed container until ready to use. These nuts will last for up to 3 months in a sealed container.

VARIATION

Try other whole nuts such as almonds, peanuts and macadamias. You could also spice them up with the addition of a ground spice of your choice at the start of the recipe. I like to use cardamom.

HONEYCOMB

Makes a decent amount that can be smashed into smaller pieces once cool

60 g (2 oz) honey
110 ml (4 fl oz) liquid glucose
300 g (10½ oz) caster (superfine)
  sugar
15 g (½ oz) bicarbonate of soda
  (baking soda)

Simple to make, this honeycomb is addictive. The recipe differs from some inferior incarnations – this actually contains honey. You'd be surprised how many don't!

The recipe calls for checking the temperature with a digital thermometer but I reckon you can ditch that and cook it by eye after you've had practice in making it a few times. You'll eventually be an expert and get the hang of it plus it's hard to correctly get the temperature without overcooking the syrup or getting your hands really hot.

This honeycomb can be packaged as a gift or used by itself or for another recipe. It is amazing dipped in milk chocolate and you must give the Milk chocolate, popcorn and honeycomb rubble a go (page 167).

Place 50 ml (1¾ fl oz) water, the honey, glucose and sugar in an over-large heavy-based saucepan. (I like to use a cast-iron pan for this, but you can use a sturdy stainless steel one instead.) Ensure the pan is much larger than the volume of the contents as the mixture will expand later on during cooking.

Line the base and sides of a 20 x 20 x 8 cm (8 x 8 x 3¼ in) square cake tin with baking paper. Liberally spray the paper with canola oil.

Heat the honey mixture in the pan over medium heat, whisking constantly. Have the bicarbonate of soda at the ready.

Cook the syrup until it starts to colour, around 155°C (311°F) on a digital or sugar thermometer. Once the temperature has been reached, turn the heat off, remove any thermometers and mix the syrup using a hand whisk.

Whisk the bicarbonate of soda in well – be careful, as the mixture will now expand furiously up to the top of the saucepan. This mixture is VERY HOT and will burn you badly if you touch it.

Lift the pan carefully and pour the honeycomb into the prepared tin using the whisk to scoop the entire honeycomb out.

Leave the honeycomb to cool for at least 2 hours before breaking it into irregular pieces.

> TIP: Add hot water to the saucepan on the stove and boil to clean and remove any stuck-on honeycomb residue.

CARAMELISED POPCORN

Makes 200 g (7 oz)

150 g (5½ oz) caster (superfine)
   sugar
40 g (1½ oz) cooked popcorn
15 g (½ oz) unsalted butter
pinch of salt

Quick, easy and delicious this stuff is so highly addictive it should come with a health warning. Try rolling the cooled popcorn in melted milk chocolate for an added layer of decadence or use it to add a crunchy element to one of your sweet creations.

Heat a large saucepan or heavy-based frying pan over medium heat and gradually add the sugar in three stages. Stir the sugar until it has caramelised after each addition, using a wooden spoon or silicone spatula. Once all of the sugar has melted and you have a deep amber-coloured even caramel, turn the heat to low before adding the popcorn and mix.

Coat the popcorn as much as you can then remove the pan from the heat. Add the butter, stir well and pour the mixture onto a baking tray lined with baking paper. Leave the popcorn to cool to warm before separating the individual pieces with your fingers.

MILK CHOCOLATE, POPCORN AND HONEYCOMB RUBBLE

70 g (2½ oz) Honeycomb
   (page 164), broken into small
   bite-sized pieces
15 g (½ oz) popcorn, cooked
400 g (14 oz) milk chocolate,
   melted

I have been a pastry chef for over 20 years and I reckon my greatest creation could be this. Three ingredients – milk chocolate, popcorn and honeycomb chunks – is all it takes to make the most addictive sweet treat ever. I sell absolutely loads of this in my shop; it's my biggest-selling confectionery item by far. Make this and take it to the cinema for the best movie snack ever.

Spray a 35 x 25 x 3 cm (14 x 10 x 1¼ in) baking tray with canola oil and line it with a piece of baking paper cut to size.

Arrange some pieces of honeycomb and popcorn in the tray. Pour most of the chocolate into the tray to cover the honeycomb, popcorn and the base of the tray. Tap the tray gently to flatten and even the chocolate.

Stud the tray randomly with the remaining honeycomb and popcorn pieces and flick the remaining chocolate over the top and again tap to flatten.

Leave the rubble to set at cool room temperature for 30 minutes. Place in the refrigerator if necessary for 15 minutes to speed things up.

Break into irregular pieces and store in between pieces of baking paper in a tin or sealed container. This will keep for up to a month if it is kept covered, but I don't think it will last that long.

PEANUT BRITTLE

Makes 700 g (1 lb 9 oz)

300 g (10½ oz) caster (superfine)
 sugar
230 ml (8 fl oz) liquid glucose
365 g (13 oz) whole unsalted
 peanuts
25 g (1 oz) unsalted butter
pinch of salt
pinch of bicarbonate of soda
 (baking soda)

This is pretty moreish stuff! The addition of bicarbonate of soda (baking soda) at the end of cooking makes the brittle not quite so hard and therefore easier on your teeth – but it's still best to try and spread it as thin as you can once it's cooked.

Peanut brittle is great as a gift as well as delicious as a garnish for a cake or dessert. Blitz it up for an ice cream inclusion or even dip pieces in chocolate.

Preheat the oven to 100°C (210°F). Spray a large baking tray with canola oil and line it with baking paper before liberally spraying the paper. Place the tray in the oven to warm it up.

Combine the sugar and 140 ml (4½ fl oz) water in a large heavy-based saucepan over medium heat and bring to the boil, stirring constantly.

Add the glucose and continue to cook the syrup, without stirring, to 115°C (239°F). Use a sugar or digital thermometer to accurately check the temperature.

Add the peanuts and cook to 155°C (311°F) over medium–low heat, stirring constantly with a wooden spoon or silicone spatula.

Remove the pan from the heat and add the butter, stirring it in, then the salt and finally the bicarbonate of soda. Stir well to incorporate.

Pour the mixture onto the warmed oven tray and use a palette knife to quickly spread the brittle as thinly as you can. Leave to cool and then break into irregular pieces.

CHAPTER FOUR

Desserts

If you are like me and you read the dessert menu first at restaurants then this chapter is for you. Have you ever wanted to produce show-stopping desserts such as the perfect soufflé, the crispiest tarte tatin or a chocolate fondant that oozes the most special chocolate filling when it's supposed to? This chapter will help you with these tasks and a whole lot more. Start off with simpler dishes, such as the dark chocolate and orange set creams before advancing to something a bit trickier like the soufflé. You'll be an expert in no time and your friends and family will love you for it.

PEAR TARTE TATIN WITH VANILLA ICE CREAM

COMPONENTS

> Vanilla ice cream
> Pear tarte tatin

This dessert is one of my absolute faves and a genuine classic – but with a twist. The crunchy pastry really makes this dessert stand out, so pay attention to the basting step in the method. This is the secret to this dessert and it ensures you have the crispiest and most caramelised puff pastry ever. Choose firm pears to ensure they don't go mushy before you finish cooking.

When testing recipes for this book, I tested this out about a dozen times for precision, but I think I'll give it another go just to make sure …

VANILLA ICE CREAM

250 ml (8½ fl oz/1 cup) full-cream (whole) milk
200 ml (7 fl oz) thickened (whipping) cream
2 vanilla beans, seeds scraped
100 g (3½ oz) caster (superfine) sugar
5 egg yolks

Place the milk, cream, vanilla seeds and scraped pods in a saucepan over medium heat and bring to a simmer. Remove the pan from the heat and set aside. Discard the pods.

Whisk the sugar and egg yolks together in a bowl until they start to thicken and pale.

Pour one-third of the hot milk mixture onto the yolk mixture and whisk well. Pour this mixture back into the saucepan with the remaining milk and cream and mix well with a silicone spatula or wooden spoon.

Cook over medium–low heat, stirring constantly, until the ice cream base reaches a temperature of 82°C (180°F). Use a sugar or digital thermometer for accuracy.

Prepare a large bowl of iced water.

Remove the custard from the heat and strain into a bowl. Set this bowl in the larger bowl of iced water, stirring regularly, to cool the custard down quickly.

Once cool, churn in an ice cream machine according to the manufacturer's instructions. Store the ice cream in the freezer until needed.

> TIPS: You can make the ice cream base up to 4 days in advance but try to churn the ice cream on the day of serving for the best possible result. >

<

Add some fresh grated ginger to the warm base and leave to infuse for an hour before straining for a warming ginger and vanilla ice cream twist.

PEAR TARTE TATIN

2 corella pears, or another firm
   variety
60 g (2 oz) unsalted butter, at room
   temperature
90 g (3 oz) caster (superfine) sugar
1 vanilla bean, seeds scraped
pinch of Chinese five-spice
   (optional)
20 cm (8 in) diameter puff pastry
   disc

Preheat the oven to 180°C (350°F). You will need a 20 cm (8 in) diameter ovenproof shallow tin or tatin tin.

Peel the pears and cut them in half lengthways. Use a corer to scoop out the core.

Spread the butter over the base of the tin and sprinkle the sugar to cover the butter. Add the scraped vanilla seeds and pod along with the Chinese five-spice, if using.

Place the pears, point towards the centre and cut side down, onto the sugar.

Place the disc of pastry over the top of the pears and tuck any excess pastry underneath the round edges of the pear around the tin. We are looking for an unfussy and rustic style appearance to this dessert, so don't be afraid to get in there and use your hands.

Using a sharp knife, cut a small slice in the centre of the puff pastry to allow steam to escape while cooking.

Place the pan on a stove, barbecue top or flame and heat over medium–high heat.

As the pan starts to heat, shake it to avoid the contents from sticking and catching.

Syrup will start to develop in the pan with the butter and sugar mixing and melting together. Use a spoon to scoop some of this syrup onto the back of the exposed puff pastry.

Get the spoon into the centre cavity and ensure an all-over liberal soaking of the pastry with the syrup. Continue to shake the pan and keep the contents moving.

Cook until the syrup turns a golden-brown colour then remove from the heat.

Place the entire tin in the oven and cook for around 20–25 minutes or until the tatin looks cooked and the pastry is crisp.

Remove from the oven and allow the tatin to cool for 5 minutes before attempting the flip.

Use oven gloves or a tea towel (dish towel) to hold a serving plate inverted over the tin, then flip in one rapid motion until the plate is on the bottom and the tin is on the top. Leave to cool for 5 minutes before serving.

TO SERVE

Cut into portions and serve the tatin immediately with some ice cream, cream, custard or all three.

> TIP: The basting of the raw pastry with the syrup might seem strange, but it is the most important part of this recipe as it ensures the pastry crisps up in the hot oven.

VARIATION

The pears can be substituted for another fruit if you wish. Try a tart including classic apple or exotic mango or pineapple. Add some spices of your choice when adding the vanilla seeds if you wish.

CARAMELISED WHITE CHOCOLATE MOUSSE, COFFEE, BANANA AND PASSIONFRUIT

Makes 4–6

COMPONENTS
> Caramelised white chocolate
> Caramelised white chocolate mousse
> Coffee crumble
> Banana ice cream

The caramelised white chocolate in this recipe is unbelievable and has the most amazing aroma and flavour. I make it by the bucketload and transform it into bars, desserts, ice creams and chocolate sprays for my cakes. It's a great technique to have up your sleeve and simple to master.

I make so much at Sweet Studio that a machine takes care of most of the hard work but, when making small batches at home, the method shown here works just as well.

I have paired the caramelised white chocolate with coffee, banana and passionfruit, which I have found work well together. However, as with all of the recipes in this book, try them as a whole or use them on their own or with your own variations to make a unique dessert combo.

CARAMELISED WHITE CHOCOLATE

400 g (14 oz) white chocolate

Preheat the oven to 120°C (250°F) and place the chocolate on a clean non-stick baking tray.

Bake the chocolate for 20 minutes then remove it from the oven.

Move it back and forth with a silicone spatula as the chocolate cools to smooth it out. The chocolate should be golden brown and have a rich caramel aroma.

> TIPS: Low and slow is the key to successfully caramelising your chocolate. Use good-quality white chocolate and remember to preheat the oven. You can open the oven during cooking to have a look and smooth the chocolate out with a palette knife or spatula. The cooking time is only a guide – you need the right amount of golden caramel colour, so cook a little longer if necessary. >

CARAMELISED WHITE CHOCOLATE MOUSSE

350 g (12½ fl oz) caramelised white
  chocolate (see above)
460 ml (15½ fl oz) thickened
  (whipping) cream
1 gold-strength gelatine leaf
  (2 g/⅛ oz), soaked and drained
  (see page 33)

Melt the caramelised white chocolate in the microwave.

Bring 160 ml (5½ fl oz) of the cream to the boil in a saucepan over
medium heat. Pour it over the melted chocolate, add the soaked
gelatine and stir gently from the centre of the bowl to the outside using
a spatula. Mix well to emulsify, ensuring you have a smooth and shiny
elastic cream.

Strain the mousse base into a clean bowl. This will ensure there are
no lumps of grainy chocolate or gelatine.

Whisk the rest of the cream to a soft ribbon stage and fold this in
gently until you have a light and smooth mousse-like texture.

Pour the mixture evenly into 4–6 serving glasses or bowls and set in
the refrigerator for a minimum of 30 minutes.

COFFEE CRUMBLE

50 g (1¾ oz) caster (superfine) sugar
50 g (1¾ oz) ground almonds
30 g (1 oz) plain (all-purpose) flour
20 g (¾ oz) Dutch (unsweetened)
  cocoa powder
10 g (¼ oz) freshly ground coffee
pinch of salt
40 g (1½ oz) unsalted butter,
  melted and cooled

Preheat the oven to 170°C (340°F) and line a baking tray with
baking paper.

Place all the dry ingredients in a bowl and mix well.

Add the melted butter and mix with your fingers to form irregular-
sized crumbs.

Scatter the crumbs on the prepared baking tray. Bake for
10–12 minutes until firm and toasted. Remove from the oven
and allow the crumb to cool. Store in a sealed plastic container
until needed.

> TIP: If you don't have fresh coffee beans or a grinder at home, you
can use the coffee from coffee machine pods. Just take a small sharp
knife and pierce the foil releasing the coffee. The weights of coffee in
pods will always be on the packets so you won't have to use scales to
weigh the coffee out.

BANANA ICE CREAM

250 ml (8½ fl oz/1 cup) full-cream
  (whole) milk
200 ml (7 fl oz) thickened
  (whipping) cream
100 g (3½ oz) caster (superfine)
  sugar
5 egg yolks
150 g (5½ oz) banana, mashed
  with a fork

Place the milk and cream in a saucepan over medium heat and bring to a simmer. Remove from the heat and set aside.

In a mixing bowl whisk the sugar and egg yolks together until they start to thicken and pale.

Pour one-third of the hot milk mixture into the yolk mixture and whisk well. Pour this mixture back into the saucepan with the remaining milk and cream and mix well with a spatula or wooden spoon.

Cook over medium–low heat, stirring constantly, until the ice cream base reaches a temperature of 82°C (180°F).

Prepare a large bowl of iced water.

Remove the custard from the heat and pour it into a bowl. Set this bowl in the larger bowl of iced water to cool the custard down quickly. Stir regularly to achieve this.

Once cool, mix in the mashed banana. Churn the mixture in an ice cream machine according to the manufacturer's instructions. Store the ice cream in the freezer until needed.

> TIPS: You can make the ice cream base up to 4 days in advance but try to churn it on the day of serving for the best possible result.

A quick way to make banana ice cream would be to just fold chopped banana into vanilla ice cream.

ASSEMBLY

fresh passionfruit pulp to garnish

Spoon a tablespoon of the coffee crumble on top of the set mousses. Add a ball of banana ice cream and finish with passionfruit pulp.

VARIATION

If you prefer, you can switch the coffee crumble for another crumble topping from this book, such as chocolate (see page 188).

DARK CHOCOLATE AND ORANGE SET CREAMS WITH MUSCOVADO STICKS

Serves 4–6

COMPONENTS
> Dark chocolate and orange
  set creams
> Muscovado sticks
> Candied orange zest

Simple and silky smooth, these chocolate pots can be whipped up in minutes and left to set, leaving you time to really enjoy that get-together with friends or family. The combination of chocolate and orange is classic and irresistible. I like to use a dark chocolate with fairly high cocoa solids as I prefer it a little bitter, but you can use any dark chocolate you wish. The muscovado sticks are a lovely textural addition and are a great scooping tool while eating the creams.

DARK CHOCOLATE AND ORANGE SET CREAMS

180 ml (6 fl oz) thickened
  (whipping) cream
180 ml (6 fl oz) full-cream (whole)
  milk
finely grated zest of 1 orange
1 egg
4 egg yolks
80 g (2¾ oz) milk chocolate, finely
  chopped
160 g (5½ oz) dark chocolate
  (65% cocoa solids), finely chopped
50 ml (1¾ fl oz) Cointreau
  (optional) or warm water

Put the cream, milk and orange zest in a saucepan over medium heat and bring to the boil. Remove from the heat and leave to sit for 10 minutes to infuse.

Return to the heat and bring back to the boil then remove the pan from the heat and set aside.

In a mixing bowl whisk the egg and egg yolks together.

Pour one-third of the hot cream and milk mixture into the egg mixture and whisk well. Pour this mixture back into the saucepan with the remaining cream and milk and mix well with a silicone spatula or wooden spoon.

Cook over low heat, stirring constantly, until the temperature of the mixture reaches 80°C (176°F), using a digital thermometer to accurately check the temperature.

Place both of the chocolates in a mixing bowl. Strain the hot custard onto the chocolate. Mix well with a spatula or whisk until you have a smooth and shiny chocolate cream. Add the Cointreau or water at this point and mix in well.

Pour the cream evenly into six dishes – I like to use wide, shallow glass bowls but anything will do. Place the dishes in the refrigerator for a minimum of 2 hours to set.

> TIPS: If you don't have a digital thermometer, then cook the custard until it lightly coats the back of the spatula.

A microplane is the best tool to use for grating citrus zests, and I prefer to zest straight into the bowl or pan, to capture all of the essential oils. >

MUSCOVADO STICKS

50 g (1¾ oz) muscovado sugar
50 g (1¾ oz) caster (superfine) sugar
1 tablespoon dark treacle (molasses)
100 g (3½ oz) unsalted butter,
  at room temperature
200 g (7 oz/1⅓ cups) plain
  (all-purpose) flour
pinch of salt
pinch of bicarbonate of soda
  (baking soda)
pinch of ground cinnamon (optional)
pinch of ground nutmeg (optional)
pinch of ground cloves (optional)
pinch of ground star anise (optional)
finely grated zest of 1 orange
2 egg yolks
raw (demerara) sugar or white sugar
  crystals to coat

Place the sugars, treacle and butter in a freestanding electric mixer fitted with the paddle attachment. Mix on a low speed until you have a smooth paste. Scrape down the side of the bowl and the paddle to ensure there are no butter lumps and mix again for a further minute.

Add the remaining ingredients, except the raw sugar, and mix again slowly until the ingredients are totally combined and you have an evenly mixed dough.

Remove the dough from the bowl and roll it out, between two sheets of baking paper, to a thickness of 2 mm (⅛ in). Place the dough in the refrigerator to chill and rest for a minimum of 2 hours.

Preheat the oven to 160°C (320°F). Line a baking tray with baking paper. Remove the dough from the refrigerator and peel off the paper. Place the dough on a chopping board and quickly cut into sticks of approximately 10 x 1 cm (4 x ½ in). Place 12 sticks on the prepared baking tray and sprinkle them lightly with the raw or white sugar crystals. Bake in the oven for 12–14 minutes or until golden brown. Store the remaining uncooked dough in the freezer for a later date.

CANDIED ORANGE ZEST

1 orange
100 g (3½ oz) caster (superfine)
  sugar
1 tablespoon liquid glucose

Peel the oranges with a speed-peeler or sharp knife. Remove any excess bitter pith with a knife and rinse the zests in cold water for a minute.

Thinly slice the zest into very thin strips and place the strips in a small saucepan of cold water. Heat the pan to boiling then drain off the water. Refresh the strips in cold water and repeat this step two more times.

After the strips have been blanched three times, add them to a clean small saucepan with 100 ml (3½ fl oz) water, the sugar and glucose and bring to the boil over medium heat. Reduce the heat to the lowest setting and cook the strips for 10 minutes. Remove from the heat and store the strips and syrup in the refrigerator until needed.

> TIP: These will last for up to 2 months, covered, in the refrigerator.

TO SERVE

orange segments
pouring (single/light) cream

Remove the creams from the refrigerator and serve with the muscovado sticks, orange segments, candied zest and pouring cream.

VARIATION

These pots can be caramelised on top as for crème brûlée. Just lightly dust caster (superfine) sugar evenly over the surface of each cream. Caramelise them briefly and evenly with a blowtorch. Once cool you will have a hard sugar crust.

You can switch orange for another citrus or spice. Alternatively you can flavour the cream and milk with green tea or Earl Grey.

PEACH MELBA

Serves 4

COMPONENTS
> Vanilla ice cream (see page 173)
> Raspberries in sauce
> Vanilla panna cotta
> Raspberry sugar shards

One of my first serious jobs as a pastry chef was my time at the legendary Savoy Hotel in London in the late '90s.

I attended an open day there before I started and a chef demonstrated how to make peach melba. He also explained the story of its creation at the hotel by Chef Escoffier around the 1890s and I immediately fell in love with the hotel and its history and was determined to be a pastry chef then and there. As this dessert is so close to my heart and knowing now that Dame Nellie Melba was an Aussie, I thought I should include my version of this iconic dessert.

It's not exactly true to the dessert shown to me 100 years after its invention, but all of the main flavours are there – with a twist.

RASPBERRIES IN SAUCE

350 g (12½ oz) raspberries
½ vanilla bean, seeds scraped
juice of ½ lemon
20 g (¾ oz) icing (confectioners')
   sugar

Place 150 g (5½ oz) of the raspberries, the vanilla seeds, lemon juice and icing sugar in a blender and blitz until smooth. Pass the mixture through a sieve over the remaining raspberries and refrigerate.

VANILLA PANNA COTTA

75 ml (2½ fl oz) full-cream (whole)
   milk
30 g (1 oz) caster (superfine) sugar
½ vanilla bean, seeds scraped
2 gold-strength gelatine leaves
   (4 g/¼ oz), soaked and drained
   (see page 33)
175 ml (6 fl oz) thickened
   (whipping) cream

Place the milk, sugar and vanilla in a saucepan over medium–low heat. Bring to the boil and remove from the heat. Stir in the soaked gelatine.

Add the cream, stir then strain the mixture into a small, clean plastic container. Leave to set in the refrigerator for 2 hours. >

RASPBERRY SUGAR SHARDS

200 g (7 oz) caster (superfine)
  sugar
1 tablespoon liquid glucose
whole and crushed freeze-dried
  raspberries (see page 13)

Line a baking tray or work surface with baking paper.

Place the sugar and 75 ml (2½ fl oz) water in a small saucepan over medium heat. Stir with a spoon until the sugar has dissolved and the syrup is boiling. Add the glucose and continue to cook, without stirring, until the caramel starts to turn an amber colour.

Remove from the heat and pour the caramel onto the baking tray or work surface.

While the caramel is hot, lift the edges of the paper to make the caramel run and become as thin as possible. Sprinkle whole and crushed freeze-dried raspberry pieces onto the caramel while still warm.

Leave to cool thoroughly before breaking into irregular-shaped shards and storing in a sealed container until ready to use.

TO SERVE

1 peach, halved

Cut the peach halves into wedges and arrange them on serving plates with the raspberries.

Take a hot spoon and scoop two pieces of panna cotta from the container and place them on each plate. Serve with the vanilla ice cream and raspberry sugar shards.

LIQUID-CENTRE CHOCOLATE FONDANTS WITH NUT BUTTER AND PEDRO XIMÉNEZ RAISIN ICE CREAM

Serves 4

COMPONENTS
> Nut butter milk (for the ice cream)
> Pedro Ximénez-soaked raisins
  (for the ice cream)
> Chocolate crumble
> Dark chocolate fondants
> Nut butter ice cream

Nail this and you'll look like a superstar. That's what really matters when having friends around for dinner – you want to be seen to effortlessly pull the night together, spending more time entertaining than stressing in the kitchen. This is so achievable, and so delicious! Get prepared and make it ahead of time. Practise before the big night to understand your oven and bask in the glory of a perfectly cooked, oozing chocolate fondant. If you have trouble though, these can be cooked and served in a serving ramekin to eradicate the element of danger. Give it a go, back yourself and get used to being a legend.

NUT BUTTER MILK

400 ml (13½ fl oz) full-cream
  (whole) milk
300 g (10½ oz) unsalted butter

Bring the milk to a simmer in a large saucepan over medium heat and remove from the heat to stand.

Place the butter in an extremely over-large saucepan over medium heat. Cook until the butter has melted and cooked past foaming and onto 'nut butter' stage. Remove from the heat and add the scalded milk in three stages. Be careful as the mixture will spatter furiously and the steam is dangerously hot.

Once all of the milk has been incorporated, pour the mixture into a plastic container and leave, covered, overnight in the refrigerator.

The next day the mixture will have separated into two mixes, a hard butter top and a liquid milk bottom. Use a sharp knife to remove the solidified butter top and strain out the infused milk liquid into a measuring jug. Reserve the butter for making pastry or greasing moulds.

PEDRO XIMÉNEZ-SOAKED RAISINS

100 ml (3½ fl oz) Pedro Ximénez
  sherry
20 g (¾ oz) soft light brown sugar
160 g (5½ oz) raisins

Put the sherry and sugar in a saucepan over medium–low heat and bring to a simmer. Pour this over the raisins in a small container, cover and leave to stand for a minimum of 24 hours.

These will last for a couple of months, covered, in the refrigerator. >

CHOCOLATE CRUMBLE

125 g (4½ oz) unsalted butter
175 g (6 oz) soft light brown sugar
125 g (4½ oz) plain (all-purpose) flour
30 g (1 oz/¼ cup) Dutch (unsweetened) cocoa powder
pinch of bicarbonate of soda (baking soda)
130 g (4½ oz) ground almonds
pinch of salt

In a freestanding electric mixer, cream the butter and sugar until smooth.

Sift the flour, cocoa powder and bicarbonate of soda into a separate bowl.

Add all the sifted and remaining ingredients to the mixer with the creamed butter and sugar and mix well to form a dough.

Spread the dough flat on a sheet of baking paper and top with a second sheet. Roll the dough to a thickness of 5 mm (¼ in), place on a baking tray and chill for 1 hour in the refrigerator.

Preheat the oven to 170°C (340°F).

Remove the dough from the refrigerator, remove the top piece of paper and bake for 12–14 minutes or until baked to golden and firm.

Blitz into a crumble in a blender or food processor.

DARK CHOCOLATE FONDANTS

Dutch (unsweetened) cocoa powder for dusting
125 g (4½ oz) dark chocolate (60% cocoa solids)
125 g (4½ oz) unsalted butter
3 eggs
2 egg yolks
55 g (2 oz/¼ cup) caster (superfine) sugar
pinch of salt
20 g (¾ oz) plain (all-purpose) flour

Chill four 7.5 cm (3 in) wide and 4.5 cm (1¾ in) deep aluminium dariole moulds or foil cups of similar dimensions for 20 minutes, then brush with softened butter or reserved butter from the nut butter milk (see page 187). Dust with cocoa powder to coat and tap out any excess from the four moulds.

Melt the chocolate and butter together in a microwave in short bursts, stirring in between each burst. (See page 141 for instructions.)

Place the eggs, egg yolks and sugar in a freestanding electric mixer and whisk on medium–high speed for 10 minutes until the mixture is pale and thick.

Turn the mixer to low speed and add the chocolate mix to the bowl until all is incorporated.

Remove the bowl from the mixer and fold in the salt and flour with a silicone spatula.

Pour the mixture equally between the prepared moulds and chill in the refrigerator for a minimum of 3 hours.

> TIPS: If you have enough moulds then make more than you need of these to do testers. They will also store really well in the freezer for a good period of time and you can cook them from frozen, which means you can just pull out what you need whenever you need them.

If you don't have the moulds or are worried they might collapse when you cook them, then you can make the mixture as above and pour it into ramekins and again store in the refrigerator or freezer to be baked from cold or frozen. Just adjust cooking times for larger portion sizes.

Use the best-quality dark chocolate that you can afford – this will show in the finished result I can guarantee. I use a chocolate with minimum cocoa solids of 60%, but choose a chocolate that is sweeter or more bitter to suit your taste.

NUT BUTTER ICE CREAM

250 ml (8½ fl oz/1 cup) Nut butter milk (see page 187)
200 ml (7 fl oz) thickened (whipping) cream
100 g (3½ oz) caster (superfine) sugar
5 egg yolks
120 g (4½ oz) Pedro Ximénez soaked raisins (see page 187), chopped

Place the milk and cream in a saucepan over medium heat and bring to a simmer. Remove from the heat and set aside.

In a mixing bowl whisk the sugar and egg yolks together until they start to thicken and pale.

Pour one-third of the hot milk mixture onto the yolk mixture and whisk well. Pour this mixture back into the saucepan with the remaining milk and cream and mix well with a silicone spatula or wooden spoon. Cook over medium–low heat, stirring constantly, until the ice cream base reaches a temperature of 82°C (180°F).

Prepare a large bowl of iced water.

Remove the custard from the heat and strain it into a bowl. Set this bowl in the larger bowl of iced water to cool the custard down quickly, stirring regularly. Once cool, churn in an ice cream machine according to the manufacturer's instructions. Add the raisins just before the ice cream has finished churning. Store the ice cream in the freezer until needed.

> TIP: You can make the ice cream base up to 4 days in advance but try to churn the ice cream on the day of serving for the best results.

ASSEMBLY

small block of dark chocolate

Preheat the oven to 170°C (340°F). Arrange four individual serving bowls or plates on a work surface and have a grater or microplane and the chocolate to hand. Have the ice cream ready in the freezer.

Remove the fondants from the refrigerator and place them on a baking tray. Bake for 8 minutes. Remove them from the oven and allow them to sit for a minute. While they are sitting, remove the ice cream from the freezer and arrange the crumble on one side of the plate.

Take a tea towel (dish towel) or cloth and gently turn the hot fondant upside down and onto the space left on the plate. The mould should come away easily and you should have a stable, cooked fondant. Grate some dark chocolate over the fondant. Place a scoop of nut butter ice cream onto the chocolate crumble and serve immediately.

> TIPS: Do a couple of practice runs to get the correct cooking times. Not enough cooking will result in a collapsed fondant when you try to unmould and don't overcook to ensure a runny centre. These can also be cooked from frozen. You need to test your oven with a couple of fondants to gauge the correct cooking time for your oven.

Sweet Essentials

FIZZY GRAPES

Wow! These are pretty special and perfect for the start or even end of a meal, they are really simple to do at home and are sure to impress your guests. All you need is a siphon gun and carbon dioxide chargers, these can be found in specialist food shops, online or from bar supply companies. These 'fizzy' grapes top off the spectacular 'Bellini' with fizzy grapes dessert on page 192. See the step-by-step technique on the opposite page, but add more grapes to your siphon if you need more than four per serve or you have more guests. Just add a splash more liquid, too.

CHARGING THE SIPHON GUN

There are two types of charging bulbs available for siphon guns. One is whipped-cream chargers (nitrous oxide) and these are for providing volume to creams, like the whippy cream stuff you find in supermarkets. The other type is a soda bulb (carbon dioxide), used for carbonating liquids such as soda (club soda) or tonic water. For this recipe, you will need the soda bulbs. You could add different flavours to grapes to create your own classic cocktail. Use black grapes for a fizzy Kir Royale with sparkling wine and blackcurrant liqueur. Or fruit purées and spices such as vanilla.

Siphon guns are becoming more popular in the kitchen these days and I've used them in a few other recipes in the book. There is a recipe on page 214 that calls for a siphon gun to make aerated chocolate. Here is another version you could try. Fill the gun three-quarters with the chocolate mixture and charge with nitrous oxide; this will aerate the mix. You can then discharge the thick chocolate mixture into a plastic container and freeze the mix, trapping the tiny air bubbles in the cold chocolate. There are many ways you can get the best out of your siphon apart from the intended use of carbonating liquids. See the aerated cream cheese foam for my Pimped up banana, chocolate and mango bread on page 203.

1 Wash the grapes and place them in a 500 ml (17 fl oz/2 cup) siphon gun.

2 Add 200 ml (7 fl oz) sparkling white wine to the siphon gun.

3 Screw on the lid of the siphon.

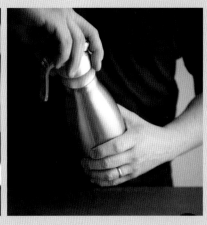

4 Carbonate with two soda bulbs. Leave in the refrigerator for at least 4 hours.

5 Discharge the liquid from the siphon gun, reserving the liquid in a jug. Don't open the siphon gun just yet though, to make sure the grapes don't fizz flat.

6 Open the siphon and pour the grapes out into a bowl. These are now ready to use for your recipe.

'BELLINI' WITH FIZZY GRAPES

Serves 6–8

COMPONENTS
> Fresh peach slices
> Sparkling jelly
> Peach and sparkling wine granita
> 32 Fizzy grapes (see pages 190–1)

This is sure to be a big hit with your guests and will make your night go with a fizz! The dish can be served at the start of the night as a livener, or as a small, cleansing course after the main before dessert proper. It includes a simple but stunning dinner party trick that's great to have up your sleeve. Serve the fizzy grapes soon after discharging, for maximum tiny bubble explosions.

FRESH PEACH SLICES

1 peach, fresh and ripe

Prepare a bowl of iced water.

Score a cross in the base of a ripe peach with a sharp knife.

Bring a saucepan of water to the boil and plunge the peach in it for 20 seconds. Remove the peach and drop it into the bowl of iced water to cool it down and prevent overcooking.

Remove the peach from the water and, using a small knife, lift the skin off the peach revealing the flesh. Cut the peach in half, discard the stone and thinly slice the halves.

Arrange the peach slices in the base and inside six to eight champagne flutes or glass bowls.

> TIPS: The peach must be ripe to ensure the skin comes off easily after poaching. Use frozen or tinned peaches when fresh are not in season.

SPARKLING JELLY

60 ml (2 fl oz /¼ cup) Sugar syrup (see page 13)
150 ml (5 fl oz) sparkling wine
2½ gold-strength gelatine leaves (5 g/¼ oz), soaked and drained (see page 33)

Place the sugar syrup and sparkling wine in a saucepan over medium heat and bring to a simmer. Remove from the heat and stir in the soaked gelatine to dissolve it.

Strain the jelly into a jug and pour it carefully and equally into the 6–8 champagne flutes or glass bowls.

Place the glasses in the refrigerator for a minimum of 2 hours to allow the jelly to set.

PEACH AND SPARKLING WINE GRANITA

125 ml (4 fl oz/½ cup) peach juice,
  purée or nectar
25 g (1 oz) caster (superfine) sugar
½ gold-strength gelatine leaf
  (1 g/¹⁄₁₆ oz), soaked and drained
  (see page 33)
125 ml (4 fl oz/½ cup) sparkling wine

Place the peach juice and sugar in a saucepan over medium–low heat and stir gently to dissolve the sugar. Remove from the heat and stir in the soaked gelatine to dissolve it. Stir in the sparkling wine. Pour the mixture into a small plastic container and place it in the freezer.

Stir and scrape the mixture with a fork every hour until you have fine shavings of ice. This may take 6 hours for the perfect consistency. Store in the freezer until needed.

ASSEMBLY

32 fizzy grapes, still in the
  siphon gun

You'll need to work fast putting this simple dish together with all of the prepared components.

Discharge the liquid from the siphon gun reserving the liquid in a jug. Don't open the siphon gun just yet though, to make sure the grapes don't fizz flat.

Remove the glasses from the refrigerator and spoon the granita equally onto the jelly in each one, leave 1 cm (½ inch) free at the top of the glass to fit the grapes.

Open the siphon and pour the grapes out into a bowl. Place three or four grapes onto the granita in each serving glass. Carefully pour the reserved liquid equally into each glass and serve immediately.

> TIPS: The juice from the siphon is delicious with the sparkling wine, taking on the extra flavour of the grapes. The grapes are best eaten as soon as they have been removed from the carbonated siphon so do this step at the last minute for maximum fizz.

*Centre: 'Bellini' with fizzy grapes
(page 192); left and right: Lime, yoghurt,
cucumber, apple, avocado and mint
(page 196)*

LIME, YOGHURT, CUCUMBER, APPLE, AVOCADO AND MINT

Serves 6

COMPONENTS
> Avocado cream
> Mint jelly
> Cucumber, lime and yoghurt
   shaved ice
> Lime curd

It's not easy being green …

This is a super-fresh and unusual dessert, wonderful as a palate cleanser or light finish to a meal. It includes a number of small recipes, which makes this dish easy to prepare, but enough to give the 'wow' factor to your guests.

I would suggest making a small portion of this dessert to serve as a cleansing course before serving a richer final dessert. It's great on a hot day and you can omit the avocado cream if you prefer – but I think it is a cool component and a great talking point for your guests.

AVOCADO CREAM

140 g (5 oz) ripe avocado flesh
pinch of salt
55 g (2 oz/¼ cup) caster (superfine)
   sugar
juice of ½ lemon

In a high-speed blender, or using a hand-held blender, blitz all the ingredients and 60 ml (2 fl oz/¼ cup) water together until very smooth. Store, covered, in a container in the refrigerator until needed.

> TIP: This component needs to be made fresh on the day. You can make it in the afternoon if you like, as it will still be fine for serving to your guests at dinner.

MINT JELLY

35 g (1¼ oz) caster (superfine) sugar
1 drop edible mint essential oil
2 gold-strength gelatine leaves
   (4 g /¼ oz), soaked and drained
   (see page 33)

Place 200 ml (7 fl oz) water and the sugar in a saucepan over medium–low heat and bring to the boil. Stir to dissolve the sugar then remove the pan from the heat.

Add the mint oil and soaked gelatine and stir again to dissolve the gelatine. Strain the jelly into a small plastic container and refrigerate, covered, for a minimum of 2 hours.

CUCUMBER, LIME AND YOGHURT SHAVED ICE

2 cucumbers
2–3 limes
125 g (4½ oz) caster (superfine)
   sugar
1 tablespoon liquid glucose
250 g (9 oz/1 cup) Greek-style
   yoghurt

Extract the juice from the cucumber using a high-speed blender or preferably a juice extractor. Juice the limes and combine the two.

Place 125 ml (4 fl oz/½ cup) water and the sugar in a saucepan over medium–low heat and bring to the boil, stirring constantly.

Add the glucose and yoghurt and remove the pan from the heat. Mix well and add the fresh cucumber and lime juices. Pour the mixture into a container and place it in the freezer.

Stir and scrape the mix with a fork every hour until you have fine shavings of ice. Store in the freezer until needed.

LIME CURD

2 eggs
juice and finely grated zest of
   2 limes
65 g (2¼ oz) unsalted butter,
   softened
100 g (3½ oz) caster (superfine)
   sugar
1 gold-strength gelatine leaf
   (2 g/⅛ oz), soaked and drained
   (see page 33)

Place all the ingredients, except the gelatine, in a bowl and whisk well to combine.

Place the bowl over a saucepan of simmering water and whisk the mixture regularly.

Continue to cook and heat, being careful of the steam, which can burn. Check your water does not run dry in the pan. Top up the water if needed. Heat the curd to 82°C (180°F), using a digital thermometer to check the temperature.

Prepare a large bowl of iced water.

Once the temperature has been reached, remove the bowl from the saucepan and add the soaked gelatine, mixing well to dissolve it before straining the curd into a bowl.

Set this bowl in the larger bowl of iced water, and stir the mixture occasionally, to cool the curd down quickly. Store in the refrigerator until needed.

> TIP: The curd can also be cooked in the microwave by placing all the ingredients, except the gelatine, in a microwave-safe bowl. Mix well and place in the microwave, cook for 20 seconds on High (100%) and stir vigorously. Repeat these steps until the curd is starting to bubble and is smooth and shiny. Remove from the microwave and add the soaked gelatine leaf. Mix well again and proceed with the method above. >

ASSEMBLY

Greek-style yoghurt
1 apple, peeled and cut into 1 cm
(½ in) dice
1 nashi pear, scooped into balls
using a melon baller
1 Lebanese (short) cucumber,
peeled into strips and curled
finely shredded mint

Beat the lime curd smooth with a spatula and spoon it equally into the base of six serving glasses.

Take a teaspoon and heat it in a cup of hot water then scoop out an irregular-shaped piece of the set mint jelly and place it in one of the glasses on top of the curd. Repeat this step with the remaining jelly in the other five glasses. (See page 35 for instructions on spooning jelly.)

Pipe or spoon approximately 1 tablespoon of avocado cream in the serving glasses.

Scoop 3 more teaspoons of mint jelly and some yoghurt into the serving glasses.

Place a few cubes of apple, balls of pear and arrange the strips of freshly cut cucumber in each glass.

Top off each of the dishes equally with the shaved ice. Place the glasses in the freezer for 5 minutes to frost up the glass. Remove and finish the dish with some finely shredded strips of mint and serve immediately.

BAKED DARK CHOCOLATE MOUSSE WITH PEDRO XIMÉNEZ JELLY AND BLUE CHEESE

Serves 4

COMPONENTS
> Pedro Ximénez jelly
> Baked dark chocolate mousse

This combination is a little fancy and a bit unusual but it all works really well together. This could be served after a main course prior to a sweeter dessert and, with the strong flavours, a little bit goes a long way. I love the bite of a salty and pungent Roquefort but you could use any blue cheese you want. Gorgonzola is probably on the other side of the scale of blue cheeses, being sweeter.

PEDRO XIMÉNEZ JELLY

180 ml (6 fl oz) Pedro Ximénez sherry
70 ml (2¼ fl oz) Sugar syrup (see page 13)
1 g (¹⁄₁₆ oz) agar agar (see page 34)
3½ gold-strength gelatine leaves (7 g/¼ oz), soaked and drained (see page 33)

Place the sherry in a small saucepan over medium heat and cook to flame off the alcohol.

Remove the pan from the heat, add the sugar syrup and whisk in the agar agar. Return to the heat and bring to the boil. Remove from the heat and stir in the soaked gelatine. Strain the jelly into a small jug through a small tea strainer.

Pour the jelly into a 30 x 20 cm (12 x 8 in) shallow, lightly greased non-stick baking tray and leave to set at room temperature for 5 minutes before transferring to the refrigerator and leaving it to set in the refrigerator for 1 hour.

Turn the jelly out of the tray onto a chopping board and cut with a sharp knife into strips approximately 8 x 1 cm (3¼ x ½ in).

BAKED DARK CHOCOLATE MOUSSE

180 g (6½ oz) dark chocolate
2 egg yolks
2 eggs
30 g (1 oz) caster (superfine) sugar
100 ml (3½ fl oz) thickened (whipping) cream, whipped
Dutch (unsweetened) cocoa powder for dusting

Preheat the oven to 150°C (300°F). Line a 20 cm (8 in) square, non-stick baking tray with a lip with baking paper (allowing some overhang) and lightly spray the paper with canola oil.

Melt the chocolate in the microwave.

Whisk the egg yolks, eggs and sugar together using an electric mixer or by hand until thick and pale. Gently fold half of this mixture into the chocolate, then fold in the remaining egg mixture.

Fold in the whipped cream. >

Pour the mixture into the prepared baking tray. Cover the tray with foil and bake in the oven for 1 hour. Remove from the oven and allow the baked chocolate to cool down entirely before chilling in the refrigerator for a minimum of 2 hours.

Use a sharp knife to loosen the edges of the baked mousse from the tray and use the excess paper flaps to lift the baked chocolate mousse out of the tin and place it on a chopping board.

Cut into 8 x 2 cm (3¼ x ¾ in) pieces, or similar, and place on a plate.

TO SERVE

small wedges or thin slices of
   ripe pear
100 g (3½ oz) Roquefort or
   gorgonzola cheese
fresh muscatel grapes

Place a piece of the baked dark chocolate mousse on each plate and leave it for 20 minutes to come to room temperature.

Arrange pieces of the jelly on the plates as well as the wedges or slices of pear.

Crumble the blue cheese over the dish and serve with the fresh muscatel grapes.

PIMPED UP BANANA, CHOCOLATE AND MANGO BREAD

Serves 6

COMPONENTS
> Banana, chocolate and
  mango bread (page 21)
> Honeycomb (page 164)
> Walnut and honey jam
> Light cream cheese foam
> Milk chocolate cream

This is a pimped-up, cheffy way of presenting the Banana, chocolate and mango bread from page 21. It shows how a new way of serving something familiar can really transform it from domestic to majestic!

With this in mind, think about how you could revamp an everyday item into something you might see in a restaurant. Using this principle of presentation, experiment with your own desserts. Try swapping the banana bread for the Light carrot cake (page 19). What would you serve with that? Have fun 'pimping up' your own puds!

WALNUT AND HONEY JAM

125 g (4½ oz/1¼ cups) walnuts,
  lightly roasted
90 g (3 oz) honey
pinch of salt

Place the nuts in a small saucepan over medium heat and cover with 500 ml (17 fl oz/2 cups) water. Simmer for 25 minutes or until the nuts are very soft.

Drain the nuts and discard the water. Place the nuts in a blender and blitz, then add the honey and salt. Blend until smoothish – add a little warm water if too thick. Set aside.

LIGHT CREAM CHEESE FOAM

200 ml (7 fl oz) thickened
  (whipping) cream
150 ml (5 fl oz) full-cream (whole)
  milk
150 ml (5 fl oz) Sugar syrup (see
  page 13)
300 g (10½ oz) cream cheese
pinch of salt

Put the cream, milk and sugar syrup in a saucepan over medium heat and bring to a simmer. Remove from the heat and stir in the cream cheese and salt.

Transfer the mixture into a 1 litre (34 fl oz/4 cup) siphon gun and charge the gun with two nitrous oxide whipped cream chargers. Shake vigorously and leave in the refrigerator for 1 hour. Shake vigorously again before use. >

MILK CHOCOLATE CREAM

220 g (8 oz) milk chocolate,
  coarsely chopped
330 ml (11 fl oz) thickened
  (whipping) cream

Put the chocolate in a bowl.

Put the cream in a saucepan over medium heat and bring to the boil. Pour the hot cream over the chocolate. Allow it to sit for 20 seconds before stirring with a spatula or whisk to emulsify. Use immediately.

ASSEMBLY

fresh mango flesh, cut into twenty-
  four 1 cm (½ in) cubes
1 banana, sliced

Spoon a small amount of walnut and honey jam into the base of each serving glass.

Place a couple of pieces of mango into the glasses on top of the jam – I use three 1 cm (½ in) cubes.

Evenly pour the milk chocolate cream into each glass. Leave the glasses to set in the refrigerator for an hour before finishing them just before serving.

Add cubes of banana bread to the glasses with slices of banana and broken pieces of honeycomb.

Discharge the light cream cheese foam gently on top of each glass and serve immediately.

CHOCOLATE-CENTRE VANILLA SOUFFLÉ WITH COFFEE SAUCE

Makes 6

COMPONENTS

> Vanilla pastry cream
> Soft chocolate centres
> Coffee sauce
> Soufflé moulds prepared with grated chocolate

'Souffle? Too hard, can't do that!' Yes you can, especially with my photographic step-by-step on pages 210–11. This dessert is extra special as it contains a soft chocolate centre and is served unmoulded.

The real secret to pulling off dishes like this is in the preparation and getting jobs done ahead of time. If I was planning to serve this dish on a Saturday night I would make the chocolate centres during the week and store them in the refrigerator or freezer. On Thursday or Friday I would make my coffee sauce and store it in the refrigerator. On the Friday I would have my moulds brushed and lined with chocolate and stored in the refrigerator. On Saturday morning I would make my vanilla pastry cream and take the eggs out of the refrigerator to bring them to room temperature.

If you're planning ahead, have a couple of practice runs on family before presenting them to friends, then you'll be turning heads with your impressive new pastry moves.

Get prepped, get ahead and get popular!

VANILLA PASTRY CREAM

300 ml (10 fl oz) full-cream (whole) milk
1 vanilla bean, seeds scraped
60 g (2 oz) caster (superfine) sugar
20 g (¾ oz) plain (all-purpose) flour
20 g (¾ oz) cornflour (cornstarch)
4 egg yolks

Put the milk, vanilla seeds and pod in a saucepan over medium–low heat and bring to a simmer. Remove from the heat and discard the vanilla pod.

Whisk the sugar, flour, cornflour and egg yolks together well until the mixture pales and thickens.

Pour one-third of the hot milk into the yolk mixture and whisk well. Pour this mixture back into the saucepan with the remaining milk and whisk well to combine.

Place the pan over medium–low heat and cook, whisking constantly, until the custard starts to boil and bubble. Cook at this temperature for a full minute, stirring vigorously the entire time.

Transfer the pastry cream to a container and store it, covered, in the refrigerator for a minimum of 2 hours and up to a maximum of 2 days.

SOFT CHOCOLATE CENTRES

90 g (3 oz) dark chocolate, chopped
125 ml (4 fl oz/½ cup) thickened
  (whipping) cream
60 g (2 oz) unsalted butter,
  softened

Place the chocolate in a bowl.

Put the cream in a saucepan over medium heat and bring it to the boil. Pour the hot cream over the chocolate. Stir until the chocolate is completely melted and you have a shiny chocolate cream. Whisk in the butter.

Leave the ganache to set at room temperature for 1 hour or so until it is thick enough for piping.

Transfer the mixture to a piping (icing) bag with a plain 1 cm (½ in) nozzle. Pipe 2 cm (¾ in) diameter bulbs of the mixture onto a tray lined with plastic wrap then freeze until firm. Once frozen place them in a plastic container in the refrigerator until needed. You will be left with more than you need, so feel free to freeze the rest for more soufflés at a later date.

COFFEE SAUCE

140 ml (4½ fl oz) full-cream
  (whole) milk
140 ml (4½ fl oz) thickened
  (whipping) cream
2 teaspoons freeze-dried coffee
  granules
3 egg yolks
25 g (1 oz) caster (superfine) sugar

Put the milk and cream in a small saucepan over medium heat and bring to the boil. Stir in the coffee until dissolved then remove the pan from the heat. Allow the coffee to infuse for an hour before re-boiling the mixture and straining it into a separate, clean saucepan.

Whisk the yolks with the sugar until a little paler and thicker and add this mixture to the saucepan. Stir to mix in well and reduce the heat to low. Cook the custard to a temperature of 82°C (180°F).

Strain this custard through a fine sieve into a jug and chill in the refrigerator for 1 hour.

SOUFFLÉ MOULDS PREPARED WITH GRATED CHOCOLATE

100 g (3½ oz) block of dark
  chocolate
unsalted butter, softened, as needed
6 metal soufflé moulds, 7 cm
  (2¾ in) diameter and 4.5 cm
  (1¾ in) deep

Grate the chocolate into a bowl using a microplane or fine grater. If the chocolate gets too warm, chill it in the refrigerator for 10 minutes.

Prepare the soufflé moulds according to the step-by-step instructions on page 210. >

SOUFFLÉ FORMULA AND ASSEMBLY

140 g (5 oz) Vanilla pastry cream
  (see page 206)
4 egg whites, at room temperature
100 g (3½ oz) caster (superfine)
  sugar
6 refrigerated Soft-chocolate
  centres (see page 207)

Preheat the oven to 180°C (350°F).

Remove the moulds and pastry cream from the refrigerator.

Place the pastry cream in a mixing bowl and smooth it out with a rubber spatula.

Follow the method for preparing the soufflé in the step-by-step instructions on page 211.

Place all the soufflés on a baking tray and pop them in the oven. Cook the soufflés for 4 minutes.

While they are baking, take six bowls and lay them out on your work surface. Pour the coffee sauce into the bowls or have it to hand in small bowls or a jug on the side.

Remove the soufflés from the oven and allow them to sit for 30 seconds before taking a cloth, picking up each soufflé and inverting them into the centre of the bowls. Serve immediately.

Sweet Essentials

CHOCOLATE-CENTRE VANILLA SOUFFLÉ

Soufflés have a reputation for unpredictability and for being tricky to get right but you really shouldn't be scared of them. The most important thing is to read the recipe through first and follow the steps carefully. You also need to have a little practice to get used to your oven, cooking times and standing times and also to ensure the maximum ooze from the chocolate centre. Make sure you have everything ready when you need it, such as prepared moulds, cold chocolate centres, room temperature egg whites and a preheated oven. This will be half the battle and the rest is easy – just whip up a few egg whites and fold and bake your way to soufflé glory.

Here are some step-by-step instructions for the soufflé recipe on page 206. These soufflés are an unmoulded variety, but you can serve them in ramekins if you wish. Just brush the ramekins the same as you would the aluminium moulds and serve them straight from the oven. This recipe uses a French meringue method, as the meringue is uncooked and therefore lighter before going into the oven.

PREPARING THE MOULDS

It is important to prepare your moulds well. Using a clean pastry brush and vertical strokes, brush softened butter into the moulds. Now add cold, finely grated chocolate to the moulds and move the moulds around so the chocolate completely covers the inside. Tap out any excess chocolate but be sure to check that the mould is completely covered. These can be prepared a day ahead.

Brush the moulds with softened butter, using a clean pastry brush and vertical strokes.

Cover the inside of the moulds with cold, finely grated chocolate. Tap out the excess chocolate, ensuring the entire inside surface of the mould is covered.

PREPARING THE SOUFFLÉS

Here are a few additional tips to the instructions below and the recipe, which will help your soufflés turn out successfully.

Make sure your tools and equipment are immaculately clean, especially the bowl and whisk you are using. Try to use older egg whites, up to 2 weeks old is great as these perform better, and make sure the whites are at room temperature as well. Mix one-third of the meringue into the pastry cream fairly vigorously, so as to loosen the thick cream before gently folding in the remainder to make sure the aeration is maintained.

Another important note is to make sure the chocolate centres are refrigerator-cold when you insert them into the soufflés. So take them out of the refrigerator at the last minute when you are assembling the soufflés.

1 Place the egg whites in a freestanding electric mixer fitted with the whisk attachment. Whisk on medium speed.

2 Gradually add the sugar in three stages. Whip until you have a firm and stiff meringue.

3 Scoop one-third of the meringue into the bowl with your pre-made pastry cream, using a spatula.

4 Vigorously blend the two together with the spatula. When you have an evenly mixed mixture, add the remaining meringue to the bowl and gently fold it into the mixture.

5 Add the soufflé mixture to the moulds, using a tablespoon. Fill to 1 cm (½ in) below the lip of the mould.

6 Push your index finger into the centre of the soufflé. Push a cold chocolate centre into the indentation. Using your finger, swirl the soufflé mixture to cover the hole.

CHOCOLATE MOUSSE WITH VIOLET ICE CREAM, HONEYCOMB AND AERO

Serves 6

COMPONENTS
> Violet ice cream
> Chocolate aero
> Honeycomb (page 164)
> Dark chocolate mousse

Everyone needs a great, simple chocolate mousse recipe up their sleeve. This one is quick and easy to prepare but silky smooth and decadent. It's a soft-set mousse for pouring into and serving from glasses or dishes, so just increase the gelatine if you are planning to unmould the mousse.

Remember to use the best-quality chocolate that you can afford for the best results. Violet colour and essence can be found online or in dedicated cookware and specialist food shops.

VIOLET ICE CREAM

250 ml (8½ fl oz/1 cup) full-cream (whole) milk
200 ml (7 fl oz) thickened (whipping) cream
100 g (3½ oz) caster (superfine) sugar
5 egg yolks
edible violet essence to taste
water-soluble violet colour

Place the milk and cream in a saucepan over medium–low heat and bring to a simmer. Remove from the heat.

In a mixing bowl whisk the sugar and egg yolks together until they start to thicken and pale.

Pour one-third of the hot milk mixture into the yolk mixture and whisk well. Pour this mixture back into the saucepan with the remaining milk and cream and mix well with a spatula or wooden spoon. Cook, stirring constantly, until the ice cream base reaches a temperature of 82°C (180°F).

Prepare a large bowl of iced water.

Remove the custard from the heat and strain it into a bowl. Set this bowl in the larger bowl of iced water to cool the custard down quickly. Stir regularly.

Once cool, whisk in the violet essence and colour and churn in an ice cream machine according to the manufacturer's instructions. Store the ice cream in the freezer until needed.

> TIP: You can make the ice cream base up to 4 days in advance but try to churn the ice cream on the day of serving for the best possible result. >

CHOCOLATE AERO

450 g (1 lb) dark chocolate, melted
   to 40°C (104°F)
50 g (1¾ oz) cocoa butter, melted
   and cooled to 40°C (104°F)

Place a couple of plastic containers in the freezer.

Mix the chocolate and cocoa butter together and pour into a warmed 1 litre (34 fl oz/4 cup) siphon gun. Screw the lid on tightly and charge with three whipped cream chargers ensuring to vigorously shake the gun in between each charge.

Discharge the mixture evenly into each container in the freezer and shut the door to let them both set hard.

After 1 hour remove them from the freezer and cut into pieces using a sharp knife. Store the aero pieces in a sealed container in the refrigerator.

DARK CHOCOLATE MOUSSE

330 ml (11 fl oz) thickened
   (whipping) cream
60 ml (2 fl oz/¼ cup) full-cream
   (whole) milk
15 g (½ oz) caster (superfine) sugar
1 vanilla bean, seeds scraped
3 egg yolks
200 g (7 oz) dark chocolate,
   chopped
½ gold-strength gelatine leaf
   (1 g/¹⁄₁₆ oz), soaked and drained
   (see page 33)

Put 80 ml (2½ fl oz/⅓ cup) of the cream, the milk, sugar and vanilla seeds in a saucepan over medium–low heat and bring to the boil.

Whisk the remaining cream to soft peaks.

Pour one-third of the cream mixture into the egg yolks in a bowl and whisk together well.

Pour this back into the pan with the cream and milk and mix well with a spatula or wooden spoon. Cook, stirring constantly, until the temperature of the custard reaches 82°C (180°F).

Put the chocolate in a bowl.

Strain the custard through a sieve into the chocolate and add the soaked gelatine. Whisk together well to dissolve the gelatine and form a smooth and shiny chocolate cream.

Use a spatula to gently fold one-third of the chocolate cream into the whipped cream and incorporate it well. Then transfer all of this mixture back into the bowl with the remaining chocolate cream. Mix well to obtain a smooth chocolate mousse mixture.

Place the mousse in a container and chill in the refrigerator for a minimum of 1 hour.

ASSEMBLY

good-quality Dutch (unsweetened)
   cocoa powder for dusting

Place some mousse on a serving plate and dust with some cocoa powder. Sprinkle some small pieces of honeycomb around the plate and top with the violet ice cream and aero.

PASSIONFRUIT PAVLOVA CLOUDS

Makes 6 clouds or 1 big pavlova

8 egg whites
pinch of salt
375 g (13 oz/1⅔ cups) caster
  (superfine) sugar
1 teaspoon white vinegar
2 tablespoons freeze-dried
  passionfruit powder (optional)
  (see page 13)
2 teaspoons cornflour (cornstarch)
Passionfruit curd (see page 221)
  to serve
sweetened whipped cream to serve
fresh passionfruit pulp to serve

These are a massive hit in my shop. We make them every day and usually sell out fast. You can omit the passionfruit powder if you can't find it but please try, as its sharp and tangy taste really works well with the sweet meringue.

These are like individual portion pavlovas and are great in your own version of an Eton mess. Simply crush the meringue and layer them in a glass with whipped cream, passionfruit curd and fresh seeds and you could serve with a mango sorbet. The quinoa crumble in the Ice cream sundae recipe (page 246) makes a great topping for this easy but show-stopping dessert.

Take a 30 x 20 cm (12 x 8 in) piece of baking paper and draw six 8 cm (3¼ in) rings evenly spaced apart. (Draw one large 30 cm/12 in diameter circle if you are making one large pavlova.)

Preheat the oven to 120°C (250°F). Grease a baking tray with a lip and place the piece of baking paper on it, circle marks down.

In a freestanding electric mixer, whisk the egg whites and salt until stiff. Gradually add the sugar, 1 tablespoon at a time. Whisk until you have a thick and glossy meringue. Fold in the vinegar, the passionfruit powder, if using, and the cornflour.

Use the largest spoons you can find, shape six equal-sized meringue 'clouds' and spoon them inside the circles on the paper. (Spoon all the mixture inside the large circle if making a large pavlova.)

If making small clouds, bake for 15 minutes. Turn the tray around and cook for a further 15 minutes before turning the oven down to 80°C (175°F) and baking for 45 minutes.

Turn the oven off and leave the door ajar allowing the oven to cool down completely before removing the clouds.

If making one large pavlova, cook for 25 minutes. Turn the tray and cook for a further 25 minutes. Turn the oven down to 100°C (210°) and cook for 1 hour. Turn the oven off and leave the door ajar to cool completely before removing.

Serve with passionfruit curd, sweetened, whipped cream and fresh passionfruit pulp.

RHUBARB, RASPBERRY AND APPLE CRUMBLE WITH GINGER ICE CREAM

Serves 8

COMPONENTS
> Ginger ice cream
> Rhubarb, raspberry and apple crumble

I adore warm fruit crumble desserts, especially in winter. I remember being happiest as a child when Mum made a piping-hot crumble with homegrown fruits and berries inside. I recall I used to burn my tongue, as I couldn't wait to dig in!

This dessert is so simple to make and the smells it produces while bubbling away in the oven are incredible. It's delicious with a big dollop of custard and a scoop of ice cream.

GINGER ICE CREAM

250 ml (8½ fl oz/1 cup) full-cream (whole) milk
200 ml (7 fl oz) thickened (whipping) cream
30 g (1 oz) grated fresh ginger
100 g (3½ oz) caster (superfine) sugar
5 egg yolks

Place the milk and cream in a saucepan over medium–low heat and bring to a simmer. Remove from the heat, add the ginger and set aside to infuse for 45 minutes.

Strain the infusion into a clean saucepan and re-boil. Remove from the heat.

Whisk the sugar and egg yolks together in a bowl until they start to thicken and pale.

Pour one-third of the hot milk mixture into the yolk mixture and whisk well to combine. Pour this mixture back into the saucepan with the remaining milk and cream and mix well with a spatula or wooden spoon. Cook, stirring constantly, until the ice cream base reaches a temperature of 82°C (180°F).

Prepare a large bowl of iced water.

Remove the custard from the heat and strain it into a bowl. Set this bowl in the larger bowl of iced water to cool the custard down quickly. Stir regularly.

Once cool, churn in an ice cream machine following the manufacturer's instructions. Store the ice cream in the freezer until needed.

> TIP: You can make the ice cream base up to 4 days in advance but try to churn the ice cream on the day of serving for the best possible result. >

RHUBARB, RASPBERRY AND APPLE CRUMBLF

350 g (12½ oz) caster (superfine)
  sugar
400 g (14 oz) (about 2) apples,
  (granny smith or golden
  delicious), peeled, cored and each
  one cut into about 8 wedges
50 g (1¾ oz) unsalted butter, melted
6 rhubarb stalks, washed, trimmed
  and cut into 6 cm (2½ in) pieces
finely grated zest of ½ lemon
finely grated zest of ½ orange
200 ml (7 fl oz) raspberry purée
1–2 vanilla beans
250 g (9 oz) frozen raspberries
500 g (1 lb 2 oz) Salted oat and
  ginger crumble, uncooked (see
  page 221)

Preheat the oven to 180°C (350°F).

Put 100 g (3½ oz) of the caster sugar, the apple wedges and melted butter in a frying pan and cook over medium–high heat. Turn the apples regularly and cook until they are caramelised. Remove from the heat and allow them to cool.

Place the rhubarb in an ovenproof dish and sprinkle over the remaining sugar, the zests, raspberry purée, 100 ml (3½ fl oz) water and vanilla beans. Cover with foil and bake for 15–20 minutes. Remove from the oven and open the foil carefully to check the rhubarb. When it is soft and a knife is easily inserted then the rhubarb is done.

Spread the cooked rhubarb, then the frozen raspberries and finally the apple in even layers in an ovenproof crumble dish.

Scatter the uncooked crumble mix onto the fruit and bake for around 30 minutes or until golden brown.

TO SERVE

Serve the crumble with the ginger ice cream.

COCONUT, PASSIONFRUIT, GINGER AND MINT

Serves 4

COMPONENTS
> Mint shaved ice
> Passionfruit curd
> Salted oat and ginger crumble
> Coconut sago

This is one of my absolute favourite dessert flavour combinations. It might sound a bit mixed, but trust me this works. The tangy passionfruit and warm ginger are cleaned off with the coconut and fresh mint. This simplified version is based on one of my best sellers at Sweet Studio.

The tangy and crunchy passionfruit and the ginger crumble are a match made in heaven when brought together by the creamy coconut and clean minty taste of the shaved ice.

The crumble mix used here is featured elsewhere in this book and I use it a lot in my desserts at the studio because it is fantastic. It's a great little recipe that you can use for a million different desserts to add crunch and bite.

MINT SHAVED ICE

1 bunch mint
120 g (4½ oz) caster (superfine) sugar
1 teaspoon liquid glucose
2 gold-strength gelatine leaves (4 g/¼ oz), soaked and drained (see page 33)
1 drop edible peppermint oil

Bring 600 ml (20½ fl oz) water to the boil then pour it over the mint in a bowl. Leave to infuse for a maximum of 4 minutes before draining through a fine sieve.

Discard the mint leaves and pour the water into a saucepan over medium heat. Add the sugar and glucose and bring to the boil. Remove from the heat and add the soaked gelatine and peppermint oil. Stir to dissolve the gelatine.

Strain the mixture into another bowl and allow it to cool at room temperature before pouring it into a shallow container and placing it in the freezer.

Break up and shave the solution with a fork every 45 minutes or so until you have complete shaved ice. Reserve in the freezer until needed.

PASSIONFRUIT CURD

2 eggs
50 ml (1¾ fl oz) passionfruit juice
   (about 2–3 passionfruit), strained
65 g (2¼ oz) unsalted butter,
   softened
100 g (3½ oz) caster (superfine)
   sugar
1 gold-strength gelatine leaf
   (2 g/⅛ oz), soaked and drained
   (see page 33)

Place all the ingredients, except the gelatine, in a bowl and whisk well to combine.

Place the bowl over a saucepan of simmering water and whisk the mixture regularly. Continue to cook and heat, being careful of the steam, which can burn. Check your water does not run dry in the pan. Top up the water if needed. Heat the curd to 82°C (180°F) using a digital thermometer to check the temperature.

Prepare a large bowl of iced water.

Once the temperature has been reached, remove the bowl from the saucepan and add the gelatine and mix well to dissolve it. Pour the curd into a bowl.

Set this bowl in the larger bowl of iced water, stirring occasionally, to cool the curd down quickly. Store in the refrigerator until needed.

> TIP: The curd can also be cooked in the microwave by placing all the ingredients, except the gelatine, in a microwave-safe bowl. Mix well and cook in the microwave for 20 seconds on High (100%) then stir vigorously. Repeat these steps until the curd is starting to bubble and is smooth and shiny. Remove from the microwave and add the soaked gelatine. Mix well again and proceed with the method above.

SALTED OAT AND GINGER CRUMBLE

200 g (7 oz/1⅓ cups) plain
   (all-purpose) flour
200 g (7 oz/2 cups) rolled
   (porridge) oats
265 g (9½ oz) soft light brown sugar
300 g (10½ oz) butter, melted
10 g (¼ oz) bicarbonate of soda
   (baking soda)
5 g (¼ oz) salt
20 g (¾ oz) ground ginger

Preheat the oven to 160°C (320°F) and line a baking tray with baking paper.

Mix all the ingredients together to form an irregular crumb. Bake on the prepared baking tray for 12–15 minutes or until golden brown. Allow the crumble to cool and break it into smaller pieces. >

COCONUT SAGO

40 g (1½ oz) sago pearls
220 ml (7½ fl oz) coconut cream
50 ml (1¾ fl oz) Sugar syrup (see
  page 13)

Place 750 ml (25½ fl oz/3 cups) water in a large saucepan over high heat and bring to a rapid boil.

Sprinkle the sago pearls into the boiling water and give them a quick stir to make sure that no pearls have stuck to the base of the pan. Cook the sago for around 10 minutes; the sago will start to go clear when cooked through.

Drain the sago through a small fine sieve when the smallest white dot can be seen in the near-translucent sago pearls. Place the cooked sago in a container with the coconut cream and the sugar syrup and stir briefly for a few minutes to cool and prevent sticking.

Store the sago in the refrigerator for a couple of hours before use to let the starches set and for the mix to become thicker. If it is too thick the sago can be thinned with more sugar syrup and/or coconut cream to the desired consistency and taste.

ASSEMBLY

fresh passionfruit pulp
4 fresh mint leaves, finely shredded

Preheat the oven to 170°C (340°F).

Place around 50 g (1¾ oz) of crumble in each of the serving glasses.

Pipe or spoon the passionfruit curd on top of the crumble to one side of each glass. Approximately 65 g (2¼ oz) per glass is a good amount but it depends on the size of your glasses.

Spoon a quantity of cooled coconut sago into each of the glasses. Tap the glasses to level slightly.

Set the glasses in the refrigerator for 1 hour before topping with the fresh passionfruit pulp, mint shaved ice and shredded mint.

CATH'S STRAWBERRY AND ROSE ROLLED PAVLOVA

Serves 8

COMPONENTS
> White chocolate, vanilla and rose cream
> Rolled pavlova
> Pistachio praline
> Strawberries in rose syrup
> Crystallised rose petals (see page 110)

My wife, Cath, is a beautiful cook and one of my greatest inspirations. She owned and operated a number of successful restaurants and food businesses and specialised in Middle Eastern–Mediterranean cuisine. Unfortunately she had a very bad experience with a business partner who put her off cooking for a while, but I am happy to say she's back! She always says she can't cook desserts but she can. This is proof of that as it is virtually the same recipe that Cath served to great acclaim at her flagship restaurant, Mecca. All I have done is reproduced it for you all to enjoy.

Thanks Cath, from all of us.

WHITE CHOCOLATE, VANILLA AND ROSE CREAM

120 g (4½ oz) white chocolate, melted
1 vanilla bean, seeds scraped
240 ml (8 fl oz) thickened (whipping) cream
35 ml (1¼ fl oz) rosewater

Put the chocolate and vanilla seeds in a bowl.

Put 80 ml (2½ fl oz/⅓ cup) of the cream in a saucepan over medium heat and bring to the boil.

Pour the hot cream over the chocolate and vanilla. Leave to sit for 30 seconds before stirring well with a spatula to combine.

Stir in the remaining cold cream. Transfer the mixture to a covered container and place in the refrigerator for a minimum of 1 hour before use.

Whisk up the cream to a thick ribbon stage using an electric mixer or hand whisk and add the rosewater. Be careful not to over-whip this cream as it can separate quickly. >

ROLLED PAVLOVA

4 egg whites
1 vanilla bean, seeds scraped
pinch of salt
180 g (6½ oz) caster (superfine) sugar
1 teaspoon white vinegar
1 teaspoon cornflour (cornstarch)
icing (confectioners') sugar as needed
365 g (13 oz) White chocolate, vanilla and rose cream (see page 225)

Preheat the oven to 200°C (400°F). Line a 30 x 20 cm (12 in x 8 in) shallow-lipped baking tray with baking paper. Spray the paper liberally with canola spray. Take two pieces of plastic wrap and lie them, slightly overlapping, on a work surface.

Whisk the egg whites, vanilla seeds and salt to stiff peaks in a freestanding electric mixer. Gradually add the caster sugar, a tablespoon at a time. Whisk until you have a thick, glossy meringue.

Fold in the vinegar and cornflour and transfer the mixture onto the prepared tray. Use a palette knife or spatula to spread the meringue evenly to the edges of the tray. Bake for 10 minutes until browned then remove from the oven. Allow it to cool in the tray for a minute or so.

Lightly dust the icing sugar onto the plastic wrap on the work surface then turn the meringue out on top of it. Remove the paper and leave to cool for 10 minutes before spreading the white chocolate, vanilla and rose cream evenly over the meringue. Use the plastic wrap to roll the pavlova into a roulade and wrap tightly. Store in the refrigerator for a minimum of 3 hours before serving.

PISTACHIO PRALINE

125 g (4½ oz) caster (superfine) sugar
1 teaspoon liquid glucose
80 g (2¾ oz) pistachio nuts, whole

Line a baking tray with baking paper.

Place the sugar and 100 ml (3½ fl oz) water in a saucepan over medium heat and cook, stirring constantly, to dissolve the sugar. Once boiling, add the glucose and cook until it just starts to go a light amber colour.

Remove from the heat and pour the caramel onto the prepared baking tray then quickly scatter over the nuts. Leave the praline to cool for 1 hour before blitzing it into a crumb using a food processor or blender. You could smash the praline in a stainless steel bowl with the ends of a rolling pin if you wish. Store the crumb in a sealed container in the pantry until needed.

STRAWBERRIES IN ROSE SYRUP

400 g (14 oz/2⅔ cups) strawberries, washed and hulled
75 g (2¾ oz) caster (superfine) sugar
squeeze of lemon juice
splash of rosewater

Put the strawberries in a bowl.

Put the sugar and 150 ml (5 fl oz) water in a saucepan over medium heat and cook, stirring, to dissolve the sugar. Remove from the heat and add the lemon juice and rosewater and pour over the strawberries. Leave to macerate for 1 hour before serving.

TO SERVE

Crystallised rose petals

Cut the roulade into eight even slices and serve with the strawberries in rose syrup, the praline crumb and some crystallised rose petals.

CHOCOLATE AND WHISKY TORTE

Makes 6

COMPONENTS
> Whisky syrup
> Drunken sponge
> Chocolate and whisky sauce
> Chocolate cream with whisky

A real chocolate-lover's dream, this dessert is definitely for adults only! We call it a drunken sponge as the texture allows it to soak up lots of the whisky syrup, leaving it full to the brim and sloshed! If you're not into whisky you can replace it with something else such as dark rum. The sponge is made and cut before being placed into the bases of six 8 cm (3¼ in) tart (flan) tins or pastry rings with a minimum height of 4 cm (1½ in) and the chocolate mixture is poured on top. You can use whatever whisky you like in this recipe, but I prefer to use a good-quality Scottish or Japanese whisky.

WHISKY SYRUP

50 g (1¾ oz) caster (superfine) sugar
finely grated zest of 1 orange
50 ml (1¾ fl oz) whisky

Place 100 ml (3½ fl oz) water, the sugar and orange zest in a saucepan and heat to dissolve the sugar. Once boiling remove the pan from the stove and add the whisky.

DRUNKEN SPONGE

2 eggs
1 egg yolk
95 g (3¼ oz) caster (superfine) sugar
2 egg whites
90 g (3 oz) plain (all-purpose) flour
10 g (¼ oz) cornflour (cornstarch)
10 g (¼ oz) unsalted butter, melted
Whisky syrup (see above)

Preheat the oven to 170°C (340°F). Line a 30 x 20 cm (12 x 8 in) baking tray with baking paper and spray with canola oil.

In a freestanding electric mixer, whisk the whole eggs and yolk with 75 g (2¾ oz) of the sugar until thick and pale. When the mixture has doubled in volume, transfer it to a larger bowl.

Clean the mixer bowl. Whisk the egg whites to firm peaks, then gradually add the remaining sugar to form a stiff and glossy meringue. Fold the meringue into the first egg mixture then fold in the remaining ingredients. Pour the mixture onto the prepared baking tray. Spread the mixture evenly using a palette knife or spatula and bake for about 12–14 minutes.

Remove from the oven and leave to cool in the tin. Turn the cooled sponge onto a work surface and use an 8 cm (3¼ in) round cutter to cut six discs out of the sponge. The remaining sponge can be used for another dessert or frozen for later use.

Use a pastry brush to dab each disc of sponge with the whisky syrup and place each soaked disc into the base of an 8 cm (3¼ in) pastry ring. >

CHOCOLATE AND WHISKY SAUCE

100 g (3½ oz) soft brown sugar
50 g (1¾ oz) dark chocolate,
  coarsely chopped
50 ml (1¾ fl oz) whisky
1 teaspoon Dutch (unsweetened)
  cocoa powder

Put the brown sugar and 100 ml (3½ fl oz) water in a small saucepan over medium–low heat then stir to dissolve the sugar. Increase the heat to medium and cook, without stirring, until you have a deep amber caramel.

Put the chocolate in a bowl.

Remove the sugar syrup from the heat and stir in the whisky. Whisk in the cocoa powder and return to the heat to cook for a further minute. Remove from the heat, pour the syrup over the chopped chocolate and stir. Strain and leave to cool.

CHOCOLATE CREAM WITH WHISKY

340 g (12 oz) dark chocolate,
  chopped
130 g (4½ oz) unsalted butter,
  at room temperature
370 ml (12½ fl oz) thickened
  (whipping) cream
40 ml (1½ fl oz) liquid glucose
50 ml (1¾ fl oz) whisky

Put the chocolate and butter in a mixing bowl.

Put the cream and glucose in a saucepan over medium heat and bring to the boil. Pour the hot cream mixture over the chocolate and butter and stir together with a spatula. Work slowly, stirring from the middle of the bowl to the outside, to ensure the chocolate has melted and you start to see a smooth shiny cream. Add the whisky and mix again.

Pour the mixture into a jug. It is now ready to use – if it becomes too thick to use, you can warm it gently in the microwave. You need the mixture fluid to set level.

Pour the mix evenly into the six rings with the soaked sponge in the base and gently tap to level. Place in the refrigerator for a couple of hours before using a blowtorch to heat the edges of the ring and unmoulding each torte onto a plate.

ASSEMBLY

Allow the torte to come to room temperature for an hour or so before dressing the dish with a scoop of any left-over chocolate cream and the chocolate and whisky sauce. You can decoratively dot the sauce around the torte on the plate if desired.

> TIP: If a slight separation appears then you can emulsify the chocolate filling with a hand-held blender until it is smooth and shiny.

WATERMELON, PEACH, STRAWBERRY AND WHITE CHOCOLATE

Serves 4

COMPONENTS
> Peach Schnapps granita
> White chocolate and vanilla cream
> Peach slices
> Sugared strawberries

These flavours work so well together and the contrast in temperature makes this beautiful to eat on a hot day.

Peach schnapps goes brilliantly with strawberries and watermelon and the creaminess of the white chocolate brings it all home. Make the granita in advance and store it in the freezer to use as a sweet and icy topping for any dessert, any time.

PEACH SCHNAPPS GRANITA

125 ml (4 fl oz/½ cup) peach schnapps
25 g (1 oz) caster (superfine) sugar
½ gold-strength gelatine leaf (1 g/¹⁄₁₆ oz), soaked and drained (see page 33)
125 ml (4 fl oz/½ cup) strawberry purée

Place the peach schnapps and sugar in a saucepan over medium–low heat and cook to gently dissolve the sugar.

Remove from the heat and stir in the soaked gelatine to dissolve it, followed by the strawberry purée. Pour the mixture into a small plastic container and place it in the freezer.

Stir and scrape the mix with a fork every hour until you have fine shavings of ice. This may take 6 hours for the perfect consistency. Store in the freezer until needed.

WHITE CHOCOLATE AND VANILLA CREAM

90 g (3 oz) white chocolate, melted
185 ml (6 fl oz) thickened (whipping) cream
½ vanilla bean, seeds scraped

Put the melted chocolate in a bowl.

Put 60 ml (2 fl oz/¼ cup) of the cream and the vanilla seeds in a saucepan over medium heat and bring to a simmer. Pour the mixture over the chocolate. Leave to sit for 30 seconds before stirring well with a spatula to combine. Stir in the remaining cold cream.

Transfer the mixture to a covered container and place in the refrigerator for a minimum of 1 hour before use.

PEACH SLICES

1 peach

Use a sharp knife to cut the peach in half. Remove the stone then cut the peach halves into slices.

SUGARED STRAWBERRIES

250 g (9 oz/1⅔ cups) strawberries
30g (1 oz) caster (superfine) sugar

Wash, hull and halve the strawberries and sprinkle the sugar over the fruit in a bowl. Cover with plastic wrap and leave out of the refrigerator for an hour or so.

TO SERVE

1 watermelon, cut into twelve 2 cm
  (¾ in) cubes

Take four bowls and distribute the strawberries evenly. Add the watermelon cubes to the bowls then the slices of peach.

Top with the peach schnapps granita and a scoop of the white chocolate and vanilla cream then serve.

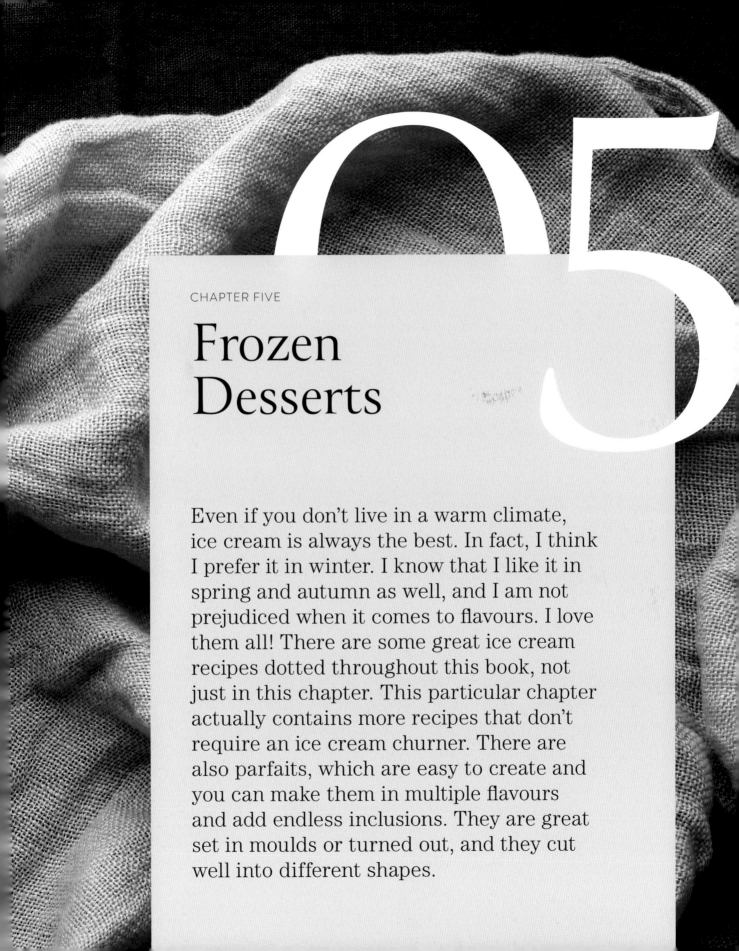

CHAPTER FIVE

Frozen Desserts

Even if you don't live in a warm climate, ice cream is always the best. In fact, I think I prefer it in winter. I know that I like it in spring and autumn as well, and I am not prejudiced when it comes to flavours. I love them all! There are some great ice cream recipes dotted throughout this book, not just in this chapter. This particular chapter actually contains more recipes that don't require an ice cream churner. There are also parfaits, which are easy to create and you can make them in multiple flavours and add endless inclusions. They are great set in moulds or turned out, and they cut well into different shapes.

LAMINGTON ICE CREAM SANDWICHES

Makes 15 with lots of yummy
bits left over

700 g (1 lb 9 oz) White and dark
  chocolate coconut biscuit dough
  (see pages 138–9), at room
  temperature
6 egg yolks
125 g (4½ oz) caster (superfine)
  sugar
1 gold-strength gelatine leaf
  (2 g/⅛ oz), soaked and drained
  (see page 33)
375 ml (12½ fl oz/1½ cups)
  thickened (whipping) cream,
  firmly whipped
six 5 cm (2 in) square lamingtons
  with jam (see recipe page 36, or
  store-bought is fine)
500 g (1 lb 2 oz) dark chocolate,
  melted
desiccated coconut for sprinkling

Wow! These are super-easy to make and you don't even need an ice cream machine. They are absolutely fantastic on a hot day and they look exactly like a regular lamington, which makes for a lovely surprise.

Spray a 28 x 18 x 3.5 cm (11 x 7 x 1½ in) baking tray with canola oil and line it with plastic wrap, allowing some overhang. Use a scraper or spatula to smooth any wrinkles from the plastic wrap.

Roll out the prepared biscuit dough on a lightly floured work surface to a thickness of 1 cm (½ in). Rest in the refrigerator for 20 minutes.

Cut thirty 6 cm (2½ in) squares from the dough, using a cutter or a knife. You may need to re-roll the dough offcuts to get 30 biscuits. Place them on a baking tray or two lined with baking paper.

Put the yolks in a freestanding electric mixer and start to whisk on high speed. Place the sugar and 100 ml (3½ fl oz) water in a saucepan over medium heat and stir gently to dissolve the sugar. Cook the syrup to 121°C (250°F), using a digital or sugar thermometer to accurately check the temperature. Once the temperature has been reached, remove the pan from the heat and slowly drizzle the syrup down the side of the bowl into the whisking egg yolks, being careful not to let it touch the whisk.

Add the soaked gelatine to the bowl and whisk for 5 minutes until the mixture has cooled. Remove the bowl from the mixer and fold in the whipped cream and lamington pieces. Transfer the mixture to the prepared baking tray and use a palette knife or spatula to push the mixture into the corners and smooth out nicely. Place the tray in the freezer overnight.

Preheat the oven to 170°C (340°F). Remove the mixture from the freezer and use the overhanging plastic wrap to pull out the parfait. Flip it onto a chopping board. Cut out fifteen 5 cm (2 in) square parfaits using a cutter or knife. Have a small bowl of hot water on hand to warm your cutter after every one is cut (or run the knife under hot water). Store the parfait in the freezer until ready for assembly.

Bake the biscuits for 14 minutes or until cooked through. Remove them from the oven and allow to cool on a wire rack. Once cool, sandwich each parfait square in between two biscuits and set aside.

Dip each sandwich in the melted chocolate and liberally roll in the coconut. Serve immediately or store in the freezer for later.

FROZEN HONEY NUT SLICE

Serves 8–10

COMPONENTS
> Honey nut parfait
> Hot chocolate sauce
  (see page 250)

Dead simple, you can have this made and in the freezer in minutes. It gets no easier than this recipe, but that's not to say it fails on taste. It's delicious and a great alternative to ice cream if you don't have your own churning machine. Slice the parfait with a sharp, hot knife for best presentation results.

HONEY NUT PARFAIT

3 egg whites
140 g (5 oz) honey
100 g (3½ oz) hazelnuts, skinned and lightly toasted, coarsely chopped
75 g (2¾ oz/½ cup) pistachio nuts, coarsely chopped
80 g (2¾ oz/½ cup) almonds, lightly toasted, coarsely chopped
50 g (1¾ oz) dark chocolate, coarsely chopped
finely grated zest of ½ orange
500 ml (17 fl oz/2 cups) thickened (whipping) cream

Spray a 30 x 12 x 6 cm (12 x 4¾ x 2½ in) or similar loaf (bar) tin with canola oil and line it with plastic wrap. Use your fingers or a plastic scraper to push out any wrinkles and smooth the edges to make sure the parfait also comes out smooth.

Whisk the egg whites in a freestanding electric mixer on high speed until soft peaks.

Put the honey in a saucepan over medium heat and bring to the boil. Remove it from the heat and pour it slowly down the side of the bowl into the whisking egg whites, ensuring it doesn't touch the whisk. Whisk until cool and then fold in the nuts, chocolate and orange zest.

In a separate bowl, whip the cream to semi-peaks and fold it gently into the other mixture. Pour the mixture into the prepared loaf tin and freeze for a minimum of 4 hours but preferably overnight.

ASSEMBLY

Hot chocolate sauce

Remove the parfait from the tin, remove the plastic wrap and slice it into 2 cm (¾ in) wide portions. Serve with the hot chocolate sauce.

> TIP: You can set the parfait in your mould of choice. You could use individual tart (flan) tins or rings lined with plastic wrap. This would mean a circular dessert that does not need to be cut with a knife to portion. Empty and cleaned yoghurt pots work well.

VARIATION

Try your own 'inclusions' in the parfait. All nuts are great, just remember to toast them, and chop them a little smaller to help with the portioning of the parfait once frozen. You can also add dried fruits such as cranberry, apricot, pear or cherry and freeze-dried fruits work really well (see page 13).

Sweet Essentials

MERINGUE

Meringue is an extremely common part of making cakes, sweets and desserts. They do have a reputation for being tricky and volatile but if you follow a few simple rules you shouldn't have any problem. Sometimes varying conditions can produce different results, such as the age and temperature of the eggs, the humidity in your kitchen and there is certainly a difference when you cook meringue in ovens you are not used to. Stick with it though – master the meringue and a world of soufflés, pavlovas and lemon meringue pies will be opened to you.

There are three main types of meringue used in the kitchen – the French, Swiss and Italian methods. They are all similar but they do have distinct characteristics, which means they are best used for different things. This book uses the French and the Italian methods, but I have also explained the Swiss method.

FRENCH MERINGUE

This is a method of meringue used to aerate mixes such as sponges and soufflés. It is a raw meringue and as such is usually used in recipes before they are baked. The raw part comes from whisking sugar into raw egg whites, which remain uncooked. The method is an easy one. Just start to whisk your egg whites and once they start to foam add a tablespoon of sugar at a time until it is all incorporated and you have a thick meringue. If the meringue collapses before the end it is probably because the sugar was added too quickly, so be sure to add it gradually.

Once ready, this can be folded into sponge batters or folded into pastry cream for soufflé (see page 211). This is the meringue used for my Passionfruit pavlova clouds on page 215 and this recipe will also make an excellent large pavlova.

SWISS MERINGUE

This type is used for piped meringue and can also be used for pavlova and dried-out meringues as well as buttercreams.

This method involves the cooking of the egg whites prior to full whisking of the meringue and is achieved by heating egg white and sugar together over a water bath. Mix the sugar and egg whites together in a freestanding electric mixer then place the mixer bowl over a saucepan of simmering water. Heat and mix by hand until the meringue base reaches a temperature of 65° (149°F). Then remove the bowl from the pan and place it back on the mixer. Whisk the meringue on high speed until it becomes thick and glossy and has cooled to room temperature.

ITALIAN MERINGUE

This is probably the most recognisable meringue as it has many uses in the sweet kitchen – and certainly in this book! For this type of meringue, a hot syrup cooks the egg whites as it aerates them, making it a stronger meringue than the other two varieties.

Uses for Italian meringue include making marshmallows (with the addition of gelatine), nougat (with the addition of honey and nuts), and glazes for cakes and frozen desserts and for piping onto desserts, such as the Lemon meringue pie éclairs on page 105.

The trick with Italian meringue is to ensure the egg whites have not been over-whipped before the hot syrup is poured on, as this will result in a grainy end product.

In order to get the best results, I have my egg whites slowly whisking in a freestanding electric mixer just before I start to boil my syrup. Once the syrup reaches 112°C (234°F), I then turn the mixer with the egg whites to medium–high speed. This ensures my egg whites are the correct texture when the syrup has reached 121°C (250°F) and needs to be slowly trickled into the mixer. Make sure you don't touch the whisk when adding the hot sugar syrup.

1 Place the sugar in a small saucepan over medium heat.

2 Add the water to the sugar in the pan and start cooking the syrup.

3 At the same time as you start cooking the syrup, add the egg whites to the electric mixer.

4 Slowly start to whisk the egg whites in the mixer.

5 Bring the syrup to the boil then continue cooking to 112°C (234°F). At this point turn the mixer with the egg whites to medium–high speed. Continue cooking the syrup until it reaches 121°C (250°F). Remove from the heat.

6 Slowly trickle the syrup into the whisking bowl, ensuring it goes down the side of the bowl and does not hit the whisk. Beat the meringue on high speed for 10 minutes to cool. The meringue should be thick and glossy.

CHOC MINT FLAKE ALASKAN SLICE

Serves 10

COMPONENTS
> Cocoa shortbread
> Frozen mint parfait
> Italian meringue

This recipe is based on two classic frozen desserts – the commercially available 'Viennetta' (which I was delighted to find was as popular here in Australia as it was back in the UK when I was growing up) and bombe Alaska.

These were seen as proper posh desserts when served at dinner parties back in the day – hilarious! I do remember them both as desserts I enjoyed immensely, so here I have combined the two, added some mint, which I love, and simplified it for home production.

See the step-by-step instructions for the assembly part of this recipe on pages 244–5.

COCOA SHORTBREAD

110 g (4 oz) unsalted butter, softened
50 g (1¾ oz) icing (confectioners') sugar, sifted
65 g (2¼ oz) cake flour, sifted
15 g (½ oz) rice flour, sifted
15 g (½ oz) cornflour (cornstarch), sifted
15 g (½ oz) Dutch (unsweetened) cocoa powder, sifted

Preheat the oven to 160°C (320°F).

Cream the butter with the icing sugar in a bowl using a spatula until pale and smooth. Fold in the remaining ingredients and mix to a dough. Wrap the dough in plastic wrap and store in the refrigerator for 30 minutes.

Remove the dough from the refrigerator and roll it out on a lightly floured work surface to a thickness of 1 cm (½ in).

Place the dough on a baking tray lined with baking paper and chill in the refrigerator for another 30 minutes.

Bake the shortbread for 18–20 minutes or until it's firm and golden. Remove it from the oven. Cut strips while the shortbread is still warm for insertion in the parfait (see page 245 for instructions). Leave to cool and reserve for assembly. >

FROZEN MINT PARFAIT

12 egg yolks
250 g (9 oz) caster (superfine) sugar
2 gold-strength gelatine leaves
    (4 g/¼ oz), soaked and drained
    (see page 33)
750 ml (25½ fl oz/3 cups)
    thickened (whipping) cream,
    firmly whipped
2 drops edible peppermint oil,
    or to taste
dark chocolate shavings (see
    page 143)

Spray a 28 x 13 x 6.5 cm (11 x 5 x 2½ in) loaf (bar) tin with canola oil and line it with plastic wrap. Smooth out any wrinkles and ensure it overhangs the tin. This will ensure you have a smooth frozen slice that is easy to remove from the tin once frozen.

Add the egg yolks to a freestanding electric mixer and start to whisk on high speed.

Place the sugar and 200 ml (7 fl oz) water in a saucepan over medium heat and stir gently to ensure the sugar has dissolved. Once the syrup is boiling, stop stirring and cook to a temperature of 121°C (250°F), using a sugar or digital thermometer to accurately check the temperature.

Slowly drizzle the syrup down the side of the bowl of whisking egg yolks, ensuring the syrup doesn't touch the whisk. Add the soaked gelatine and whisk for 5 minutes until the gelatine has dissolved and the mixture has cooled. The mixture should be pale and thick in volume.

Remove the bowl from the mixer and fold in the whipped cream and peppermint oil to taste.

Place some dark chocolate shavings into the prepared tin and pour in one-third of the parfait mixture. Arrange some pieces of chocolate shavings inside, lengthways, followed by some shortbread.

Add another one-third of the parfait and again some chocolate shavings and some shortbread before pouring the remainder of the parfait into the tin.

Cover with plastic wrap and freeze for a minimum of 4 hours but preferably overnight.

To unmould, gently warm the sides of the tin with your hands and pull the plastic wrap out. Remove the parfait and invert it onto a tray or chopping board. Remove the plastic wrap and store in the freezer until ready to use.

ITALIAN MERINGUE

200 g (7 oz) caster (superfine)
 sugar
4 egg whites

See the step-by-step instructions on page 239 for making Italian meringue.

Place the sugar and 150 ml (5 fl oz) water in a small saucepan over medium heat.

At the same time add the egg whites to a freestanding electric mixer and start to whisk them slowly on low speed.

Bring the syrup to the boil then continue cooking until the syrup reaches 112°C (234°F), using a digital or sugar thermometer for accuracy, before turning the electric mixer to medium–high speed.

When the syrup reaches 121°C (250°F), remove the pan from the heat and slowly drizzle the syrup down the side of the whisking bowl, making sure it does not hit the whisk.

Once all the syrup is in, beat the meringue on high speed for 10 minutes to cool. The meringue should be thick and glossy.

ASSEMBLY

Use a palette knife or spatula to spread the meringue over the entire parfait.

Use a blowtorch to lightly glaze the meringue all over then serve.

Sweet Essentials

ASSEMBLING THE CHOC MINT FLAKE ALASKAN SLICE

Here are some step-by-step assembly instructions to help you create the recipe on page 241. The loaf (bar) tin used here is first sprayed with canola oil then lined with plastic wrap. Greasing the tin means the plastic wrap will stick to the inside of the tin but your fingers can get it right into the corners and smooth out any wrinkles. The plastic wrap is also used to help remove the parfait from the tin once frozen. It's important that the chocolate used in the parfait is flaked as shown and not too thick. If it's too thick it will be difficult to slice through when frozen. Try to make space in your freezer before you need it. I did this by consolidating my bottom and top shelves and removing one of them.

1 Place some dark chocolate shavings into the prepared tin.

2 Pour one-third of the parfait mixture into the tin.

3 Arrange some chococlate shavings inside the tin, lengthways, followed by some shortbread.

4 Top with another one-third of the parfait mixture.

5 Again add some chocolate shavings and shortbread. Pour the remainder of the parfait into the tin.

6 Cover with the plastic wrap and freeze for 4 hours or overnight. Unmould the parfait using the plastic wrap to help.

7 Invert the parfait onto a chopping board. Remove the plastic wrap and spoon the meringue on top.

8 Use a palette knife or spatula to spread the meringue over the entire parfait.

9 Use a blowtorch to lightly glaze the meringue all over before serving.

ICE CREAM SUNDAE

COMPONENTS

> Puffed quinoa, orange and malt crumble
> Variable (but see Assembly below)

I really like desserts in tall glasses filled with layered sweet explosions and surprises. Anything works in this dessert really, and it's a fun and simple get together of a few dessert elements from this book – all topped off with an amazingly delicious crumble made from puffed quinoa. It's modelled beautifully by chocolatier Christean Ng, who does amazing work at Sweet Studio.

PUFFED QUINOA, ORANGE AND MALT CRUMBLE

100 g (3½ oz/⅔ cup) plain (all-purpose) flour
100 g (3½ oz) puffed quinoa
100 g (3½ oz) soft light brown sugar
35 g (1¼ oz) muscovado sugar
1 teaspoon bicarbonate of soda (baking soda)
½ teaspoon salt
10 g (¼ oz) malt powder
finely grated zest of 1 orange
150 g (5½ oz) unsalted butter, melted and cooled

Preheat the oven to 160°C (320°F). Line a baking tray (or two) with baking paper.

Mix all the ingredients, except the butter, together in a bowl. Add the cooled melted butter and mix well until you have a coarse crumb.

Scatter the crumbs onto the prepared baking tray/s and bake in the oven for 16–20 minutes. Remove from the oven, cool and store in a sealed container until needed.

> TIP: Puffed quinoa and malt powder will both be available from health food stores and now in some supermarkets. If you can't find malt powder, try substituting it with a malt drink powder.

ASSEMBLY

Salted caramel (page 94)
Lamington chunks (see page 36)
Raspberry jam (page 52)
Vanilla ice cream ball (see page 173)
Dark chocolate and nut brownie chunks (page 27)
Violet ice cream ball (see page 213)
Honeycomb chunks (page 164)
Chocolate ice cream (see page 22)
Raspberry marshmallow bulbs (see page 79)
Puffed quinoa, orange and oat crumble (see recipe above)
Hot chocolate sauce (see page 250)

Layer all of the desserts on top of each other in the order listed.

ROAST PUMPKIN ICE CREAM WITH COFFEE CRUMBLE AND HOT CHOCOLATE SAUCE

Serves 4 or more

COMPONENTS
> Caramelised pepitas
> Roast pumpkin ice cream
> Coffee crumble (see page 178)
> Hot chocolate sauce

This is ideal for a Halloween-themed dinner party, or just during the winter when pumpkins are at their best and desserts seem like a necessity to get you through the short days.

This may sound like an unusual flavour pairing, but the warming, roasted notes of the pumpkin ice cream really suit the 'pop' of coffee – and nearly everything goes well with a hot chocolate sauce.

The pepitas (pumpkin seeds) provide a crunch and are pretty good in salads too!

CARAMELISED PEPITAS

130 g (4½ oz) caster (superfine) sugar
1 teaspoon liquid glucose
150 g (5½ oz/1 cup) pepitas (pumpkin seeds)

Preheat the oven to 180°C (350°F).

Place 80 ml (2½ fl oz/⅓ cup) water and the sugar in a saucepan over medium heat and bring the syrup to the boil. Stir gently to dissolve the sugar before adding the glucose. Add the pepitas and cook for 1 minute before draining the syrup and reserving the seeds.

Place the seeds on a baking tray lined with baking paper and cook in the oven for 10 minutes or until the seeds are glossy and crisp.

Remove the seeds from the oven and leave them to cool. When the seeds are still warm but not hot, use your hands to separate them. Store the seeds in a sealed container until ready to use.

ROAST PUMPKIN ICE CREAM

250 g (9 oz) pumpkin (winter squash), peeled and seeded
250 ml (8½ fl oz/1 cup) full-cream (whole) milk
200 ml (7 fl oz) thickened (whipping) cream
1 vanilla bean, seeds scraped
100 g (3½ oz) caster (superfine) sugar
5 egg yolks

Preheat the oven to 200°C (400°F).

Wrap the pumpkin in foil and bake in the oven for 30–35 minutes or until soft. Open the foil and put the pumpkin back in the oven for a further 10 minutes to crisp up some edges.

Place the milk, cream, vanilla seeds and pod in a saucepan over medium–low heat and bring to a simmer. Remove from the heat and set aside. Discard the vanilla pod.

In a mixing bowl whisk the sugar and egg yolks together until they start to thicken and pale. >

<

Pour one-third of the hot milk mixture into the egg yolk and sugar mixture and whisk well. Pour this mixture back into the saucepan with the milk mixture and mix well with a silicone spatula or wooden spoon. Place the pan back over medium–low heat and stir the ice cream base constantly until the temperature reaches 82°C (180°F), using a digital thermometer for accuracy.

Remove the custard from the heat and pour it into a jug.

Place the roasted pumpkin in a blender and start to blend to a purée. Trickle the ice cream base into the blender to help the purée to smooth out. Continue to add the ice cream base until it has all been incorporated.

Prepare a large bowl of iced water.

Pour the pumpkin ice cream base into a bowl and set this bowl in the larger bowl of iced water to cool it down quickly.

Once cool, churn in an ice cream machine according to the manufacturer's instructions. Store the ice cream in the freezer until needed.

> TIP: You can make the ice cream base up to 4 days in advance, but try to churn the ice cream on the day of serving to achieve the best possible result.

HOT CHOCOLATE SAUCE

75 ml (2½ fl oz) thickened
  (whipping) cream
75 ml (2½ fl oz) full-cream (whole)
  milk
20 g (¾ oz) caster (superfine) sugar
150 g (5½ oz) dark chocolate,
  roughly chopped

Place the cream, milk and sugar in a saucepan over medium heat and bring to the boil. Remove from the heat and stir in the chocolate. Stir to a smooth sauce and serve immediately.

ASSEMBLY

Spoon some coffee crumble onto a serving plate – this is a textural element and also stops the ice cream from slipping around.

Shape or spoon the ice cream onto the crumble and top with a few of the caramelised pepitas.

Serve the hot chocolate sauce on top or in a jug on the side.

VANILLA ICE CREAM WITH BAKED PLUM, SABLÉ AND SOFT CHEESE

Serves 4

COMPONENTS
> Vanilla ice cream (see page 173)
> Gold-encrusted smoked
  vanilla salt flakes
> Baked plum
> Sablé Breton
> Pont-l'Évêque cheese

Cheese with ice cream? This may sound like a strange combination, but the salty, strong taste of the cheese works really well with the sweet vanilla ice cream. Paired with bitey sablé biscuit and the relief of the fruit, it is an amazing little dish, which is straightforward to prepare and acts as a cheeky cheese course between the last savoury dish and dessert proper.

GOLD-ENCRUSTED SMOKED VANILLA SALT FLAKES

smoked salt flakes
scraped vanilla seeds
edible gold lustre

Place all the ingredients together in a small plastic container and shake well to disperse and mix. Do this a minimum of 4 hours prior to using.

BAKED PLUM

1 plum
20 g (¾ oz) soft light brown sugar

Preheat the oven to 160°C (320°F).

Cut the plum in half and remove the stone. Cut the halves into quarters. Place the plum quarters, cut side up, on a baking tray and sprinkle them with the brown sugar.

Bake the plum pieces in the oven for 20 minutes. Remove them from the oven and allow to cool. Use a spoon to scoop out the flesh leaving behind the skins. >

SABLÉ BRETON

2 egg yolks
80 g (2¾ oz/⅓ cup) caster
  (superfine) sugar
110 g (4 oz/¾ cup) plain
  (all-purpose) flour
1 teaspoon baking powder
pinch of salt
80 g (2¾ oz) unsalted butter,
  at room temperature

Beat the egg yolks and sugar with an electric mixer until thick and pale.

Sift the flour and baking powder together in a bowl and add the salt.

Whisk the butter into the egg yolk and sugar mixture and remove the bowl from the mixer. Fold in the flour mixture and mix until you have a paste.

Transfer the mixture onto a sheet of baking paper. Place a second sheet on top and roll the paste to a 1 cm (½ in) thickness. Chill the dough for 1 hour in the refrigerator.

Preheat the oven to 165°C (330°F).

Remove the dough from the refrigerator and remove the top sheet of paper while the dough is cold. Place the sablé on a baking tray.

Bake the sablé for 15 minutes or until golden brown. Remove the sablé from the oven and allow it to cool slightly before breaking it into irregular-sized crumbs. Keep warm for assembly.

ASSEMBLY

80–90 g (2¾–3 oz) ripe Pont-
  l'Évêque cheese, or any other
  soft cheese

Sprinkle the warm sablé onto serving plates and place a piece of very soft cheese next to it. Add pieces of cooled plum and a scoop of ice cream. Sprinkle a few smoked vanilla salt flakes onto the ice cream and then serve immediately.

Index

Page number in *bold italic* indicate a recipe photo that does not occur alongside the relevant recipe.

Five minutes with Darren Purchese

One of my earliest food memories is picking wild raspberries, strawberries, blackberries and gooseberries from bramble bushes near my house in Guildford, Surrey, in the UK. I remember fruit crumbles with custard – and I still love them. I also recall boiled eggs with buttery soldiers and even now I like too much butter on my bread. I remember a special dinner for Dad's birthday when I was young and Mum making a dish with fillet steak and lobster, which I thought was the best thing ever, and I felt very sophisticated eating it. I think it probably cost them an arm and a leg.

My first job in a professional kitchen was washing up in a resort in Greece, in the coastal southern Peloponnese, in the '90s. By the end of the season, I was cooking. I returned to the UK telling everyone I was a chef and started to give Mum tips on how to cook the family meal. She was not impressed.

I do have a sweet tooth. I remember family holidays in Spain and my sister Emma and I being so excited to order dessert at the restaurants. We ordered things like knickerbocker glory, orange sorbets served in halved-out oranges and, of course, chocolate desserts. I remember we were allowed to stay up late on those nights and sometimes desserts with sparklers arrived at our table and we loved them. They are happy memories that sparked a love for theatrical and sweet finishes to a meal.

Mum and Dad had a clue for my passion for cooking at an early age. I used to make a mean cheese on toast (still do) and I would put extra toppings on store-bought pizzas because I thought I was being creative. I would give my opinion during family cooking times and was always open to new ingredients and flavours. Broad (fava) beans were a favourite of mine as a toddler.

Chocolate is my favourite ingredient, whether dark, milk or white. Did you guess? White chocolate is knocked by snobs, but I believe it is one of the most underrated ingredients. It carries flavours and infusions so well.

In many ways, *Lamingtons & Lemon Tart* is representative of my life in cooking so far. I love lemon tarts and spent a large part of my early years in pastry kitchens perfecting them. When I moved to Australia, more than a decade ago, I had no idea what a lamington was. But I am now a convert – and a huge fan. You see them increasingly in the UK, too. I hope I can help bring the lamington to the world – people don't know what they're missing out on.

Hands down, the most popular cake at Burch & Purchese Sweet Studio is my explosive raspberry creation. It has a chocolate-chip cookie base, exaggerated raspberry cream, raspberry compote, raspberry marshmallow, raspberry and milk chocolate mousse, milk chocolate glaze, chocolate-coated popping candy and freeze-dried raspberries. Phew! The flavours are recreated in my Explosive raspberry wagon wheels on page 147.

My wife, Cath Claringbold, is an accomplished chef herself. Ask me what I've learned from her and the answer is, 'Pretty much everything!' She has taught me a lot about Middle Eastern food and food in general. We make a great team.

I've learned so much in the five years of my business at Sweet Studio on Chapel Street, in (Melbourne's) South Yarra. First, the importance of listening to my customers. Also, that there is no shortcut to success. I have learned that you can do anything if you put your mind to it. I have discovered that I am part of a lucky minority of people who can work with their partner. I have also learned that 209 is the minimum number of songs on a playlist that you must have if you are to listen to that playlist every day for five years and not get sick of it (all of our songs in the shop have a sweet connotation – find me on Spotify to check out our Sweet Studio playlist.)

Being asked to name a favourite recipe in this book is like being asked to name your favourite child. It's hard, but truth is, I probably use my tangy lemon curd more often than most other recipes. I just love the tang. The tarte tatin (page 173) is a dinner party winner, too, and I also am very happy to pass on one of my most closely guarded secrets – my salted caramel (page 94).

My advice for novice bakers would be to plan ahead. Work out what recipe you're going to make, then read it through from start to finish. Get all the ingredients and weigh them precisely. Ensure you have the right equipment and preheat your oven. Enjoy and cook with love and care.

My ultimate dinner (excluding friends and family, of course) would be with a bunch of lads from home. Maybe Paul Weller, Ian Brown (Stone Roses), Ian Botham, Bobby Moore (England's World Cup-winning captain), Shaun Ryder (Happy Mondays), Joe Strummer (The Clash), Columbo, Idris Elba, George Harrison, Tony Hadley, David Beckham and Noel Gallagher. We would have drinks then dinner somewhere like Vue de Monde (Shannon Bennett's restaurant in Melbourne) – and then on to a club.

Find me on social media
(@darrenpurchese or @burchpurchese).
And say hi!

Thanks

I would love to extend my thanks to the following people, for all their help, support, advice, guidance and inspiration in making this book.

My wife, Cath (spiced apple cake model); Mum and Dad (Shirley and Don); my sister Emma Novashinski; Trish and Ken Claringbold; Tony and Marg; Libby, Tom and Aaron.

Book people: The entire team at Hardie Grant Books including Jane Willson, Mark Campbell, Vaughan Mossop, Ariana Klepac, Emily O'Neill and Susanne Geppert.

Photos and styling (A Team) – glass of champagne?: Patricia Niven, Rich MacDonald and Leesa O'Reilly.

#teamdarrenpurchese: CJ (Charlotte James, communications); Joe Chahin and the team at BR Wellington; Peter Bazzani; Rachel Reed and Bree Laughlin (thank you for beautifully modelling my choux bun); Fiona Maurer; Ari Hatzis; Kate Mansell; Sue and Richard Harris; Dave, Kirsty, Archie, Connor and Jessica Harris; Mike, Liz, Sophie and Ava Harris; Matty, Claire, Olie, Oscar and Arthur; Liam, Debbie, Ruby and Alex O'Mahoney; Duncan Stone; Mouse, Deb and boys.

#teamburchpurchese: Christean Ng (modelling the ice cream sundae); Tia Ridgewell; Nichole Horvath (swiss roll Nichole); Ryan Byrne and daughter Mitsuki Byrne (modelling my chocolate milk); Simon Docherty; Julian Ardolino; Freya Schellhorn.

Suppliers and friends: Fiat Chrysler Australia; Duncan Black and David Van Rooy – Vanrooy Machinery; Nespresso; Cancer Council Australia; The Langham, Melbourne; Mat and Vanessa – Rooftop Honey; Tommy Roff – Fresh-As; Bart Zagame and Phil Baressi – Creative Ingredients; Rob Iannantuono – Campania; Pascal – F Mayer.

Special thanks to Matt Preston for the foreword.

Finally, thank you to all of my supporters.

Published in 2016 by Hardie Grant Books

Hardie Grant Books (Australia)
Ground Floor, Building 1
658 Church Street
Richmond, Victoria 3121
www.hardiegrant.com.au

Hardie Grant Books (UK)
5th & 6th Floors
52-54 Southwark Street
London SE1 1UN
www.hardiegrant.co.uk

A Cataloguing-in-Publication entry is available from the catalogue
of the National Library of Australia at www.nla.gov.au

LAMINGTONS & LEMON TART
ISBN: 9781743791868

Publishing Director: Jane Willson
Project Editor: Ariana Klepac
Design Managers: Mark Campbell, Vaughan Mossop
Designer: Emily O'Neill
Typesetter: Susanne Geppert
Photographer: Patricia Niven
Stylist: Leesa O'Reilly
Production Manager: Todd Rechner

Colour reproduction by Splitting Image Colour Studio

Printed in China by 1010 Printing International Limited

Find this book **Cooked.**
cooked.com.au | cooked.co.uk